Excel for iPad & iPad Pro

SEAN KELLS

Questing Vole Press

Excel for iPad & iPad Pro
by Sean Kells

Copyright © 2016 by Questing Vole Press. All rights reserved.

Editor: Walt Rodale
Proofreader: Diane Yee
Compositor: Kim Frees
Cover: Questing Vole Press

Contents

1 Getting Started with Excel for iPad 1
   Office 365 Subscriptions 2
   iPad Basics 4
   Using Multitouch Gestures 6
   Getting Excel 7
   Working with Excel 8

2 Storing, Sharing, and Printing Files 15
   Local Storage on Your iPad 16
   Cloud Storage on OneDrive 19
   Working Offline 21
   Resolving Editing Conflicts 23
   Sharing Files 24
   Printing Files 26

3 Spreadsheet Basics 27
   The Excel Workspace 28
   Supported File Types 30
   Workbooks 31
   Worksheets 38
   Cells, Rows, and Columns 41

4 Entering and Formatting Data 51
   Editing Cells 52
   Using an External Keyboard 56
   Using Editing Tools 57
   Working with Comments 58
   Formatting and Styling Cells 59
   Wrapping Text in a Cell 63
   Cutting, Copying, and Pasting Cells 64
   Merging Cells 66
   Filling Cells with Data Series 68
   Sorting Data 70

5 Formulas and Functions 71
Formula Basics 72
Parts of a Formula 74
Entering Formulas 76
Evaluation Order 78
Cell References 79
Comparison Operators 85
Functions 88
AutoSum 92
Copying and Moving Formulas 94
Correcting Common Formula Errors 98

6 Tables 101
Table Basics 102
Creating a Table 104
Formatting a Table 106
Working with a Table 108
Using the Total Row 110
Sorting a Table 111
Filtering a Table 112
Using Formulas in a Table 113

7 Charts 115
Chart Basics 116
Picking a Chart Type 119
Creating a Chart 124
Formatting a Chart 126

8 Pictures, Shapes, Text Boxes, and Add-Ins 129
Creating Objects 130
Working with Pictures 131
Working with Shapes and Text Boxes 132
Working with Add-Ins 134

Index 135

CHAPTER 1

Getting Started with Excel for iPad

Excel is the spreadsheet application in Microsoft's **Office** suite for iPad. (Other Office apps include Word for word processing, PowerPoint for presentations, Outlook for email, and OneNote for note-taking.) Office for iPad apps all look and act consistently, and retain the design elements of Microsoft Office for Windows while following Apple's guidelines for native iPad apps.

Office 365 Subscriptions

Excel, like all Office apps, is free to download from Apple's App Store. After you sign in with a Microsoft account, you can use Excel's **core features** for free: you can create, view, and print workbook files (*workbook* is Excel lingo for "spreadsheet"), and perform most editing tasks.

Premium features

To use Excel's **premium features** (in addition to the core features), you must buy an **Office 365** subscription from Microsoft. Premium features include:

- Customize PivotTable styles and layouts
- Add custom colors to shapes
- Insert and edit WordArt
- Add shadows and reflection styles to pictures
- Add and modify chart elements

Tip: For a list of premium features and qualifying Office 365 subscriptions, go to *products.office.com/office-resources*.

Types of Office 365 subscriptions

Office 365 subscriptions are available on a monthly or yearly basis, and the first 30 days is free. You can buy a subscription within Excel for iPad (or any other Office for iPad app) by tapping Upgrade in backstage view (page 11), but you're better off going to *office.com/try* in a browser to see all your options (Figure 1.1).

Office 365 subscription plans are available for individuals, students, households, and businesses. Terms and prices vary by plan, but every plan lets you:

- Install and run all Office applications on a fixed (maximum) number of Windows PCs, Macs, tablets, and smartphones.
- Store, sync, and share files online on OneDrive, Microsoft's cloud service.
- Download and install all Office software updates, which Microsoft releases on a rolling basis.

Tip: If you subscribe to Office 365 as an **in-app purchase** within an Office for iPad app, Apple takes a 30% cut of your money. If you sign up on the office.com website, Microsoft gets all your money.

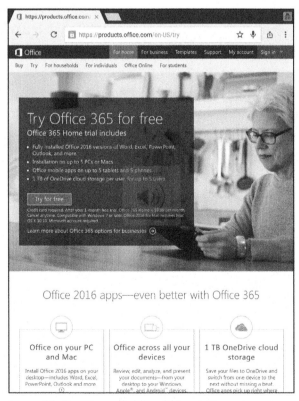

Figure 1.1 The Microsoft Office 365 website.

Excel for iPad Features Overview

Excel for iPad fills the gap between the full-featured desktop versions of Excel for Windows or Mac and the limited versions that run on smartphones or web browsers. Excel for iPad features covered in this book include:

- Subscribe to Office 365 and install Microsoft Office apps on multiple computers and tablets.
- Sign in to Excel with your Microsoft account or Office 365 account.
- Manage your files in backstage view.
- Use the ribbon to find commands quickly.
- Store your files locally on your iPad or in the cloud on OneDrive.
- Use OneDrive to store, share, sync, or collaborate on workbooks online.
- Access files stored on Dropbox or iCloud Drive.
- Work on cloud-based workbooks even when you're offline.
- Resolve editing conflicts for workbooks that have multiple authors.
- Share and print your files.
- Export workbooks in PDF format.
- Transfer files between your iPad and computer.
- Create workbooks based on Microsoft's professionally designed templates.
- Organize your workbooks in folders.
- Add multiple worksheets to your workbooks.
- Work with worksheet cells, rows, and columns.
- Edit and format cells and use the built-in editing tools.
- Add and edit comments in a workbook.
- Cut, copy, paste, merge, fill, and sort cells.
- Enter, copy, move, and troubleshoot formulas.
- Choose from more than 340 built-in functions and operators to build formulas.
- Sum rows or columns of numbers automatically.
- Calculate summary statistics without using formulas.
- Organize your data in a table to simplify sorting, filtering, and other common tasks.
- Chart your data to reveal trends and relationships.
- Embellish your workbooks with pictures, shapes, text boxes, and add-ins.

iPad Basics

This section reviews the iPad's Home screen and multitouch gestures. If you need a refresher on other basics, such as syncing with iTunes or connecting to the internet, then refer to the *iPad User Guide* at *help.apple.com/ipad*.

Tip: The text under app icons can be hard to read, particularly with lighter-colored wallpapers; to make the text bold, tap Settings > General > Accessibility > Bold Text. To turn off the 3D parallax effect that makes icons and alerts "float" above the wallpaper when you twist your iPad in space, tap Settings > General > Accessibility > Reduce Motion > On.

The Home screen

After you unlock your iPad, the **Home screen** appears and displays icons for your **applications**, or **apps** (Figure 1.2). The iPad comes with built-in apps (Safari, Mail, and Settings, for example) and you can download more—including Excel—from the App Store, Apple's online store for iOS applications. If you install lots of apps, new Home screens sprout automatically to display their icons. Put your most frequently used apps in the **dock**, which is visible at the bottom of every Home screen. The row of small **indicator dots** above the dock indicates how many screens you have and which one you're on. (You can create up to 11 Home screens.) You can customize the layout of app icons on the Home screen and in the dock.

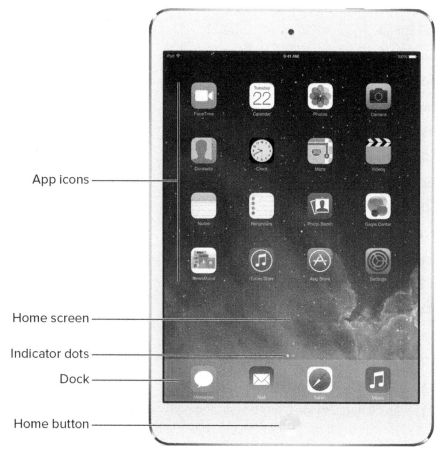

Figure 1.2 The Home screen.

4 Excel for iPad & iPad Pro

Multitasking

On an iPad, you can use four or five fingers to:

- Pinch to the Home screen
- Flick up to show the multitasking screen
- Flick left or right to switch apps

You can also multitask by using the following features on a newer iPad running iOS 9 or later:

- **Slide Over** overlays a narrow view on the right side of the screen that lets you open a second app without leaving the one you're in. To invoke Slide Over, flick or drag leftward from the right edge of the screen. To open a different secondary app, flick or drag downward from the top edge of the screen on the right side (above the current secondary app), and then tap an app in the list that appears. To dismiss the Slide Over view and get back to the app that you were using before, tap or flick to the left of the Slide Over view.

- **Split View** displays two side-by-side apps, letting you view, resize, and interact with both of them. To invoke Split View, enter Slide Over and then tap or drag the vertical divider control near center screen. Drag the divider left or right to resize the apps, or drag it all the way to the left or right to dismiss one of the apps.

- **Picture in Picture** (sometimes called PiP) lets you play video in a moveable, resizable, mini-window that floats over other open apps. To invoke Picture in Picture, press the Home button while you're playing video (in FaceTime or the Videos app, for example). The video window scales down to a corner of your screen. Tap to open a second app, and your video continues to play while you use the other app.

Tip: To toggle multitasking features, tap Settings > General > Multitasking.

To show the Home screen:

- Do any of the following:
  - ▶ Press the Home button.
  - ▶ Use four or five fingers to pinch to the Home screen.

To switch Home screens:

- Do any of the following:
  - ▶ Flick left or right.
  - ▶ Tap to the left or right of the indicator dots above the dock.
  - ▶ To go to the first Home screen, press the Home button.

To rearrange Home-screen icons:

1. Touch and hold any app icon for a few seconds until all the icons wiggle.
2. Drag icons to new locations within a screen or off the edge of one screen and onto the next.
3. Press the Home button to stop the wiggling and save your arrangement.

To reset the Home screen to its original layout:

- Tap Settings > General > Reset > Reset Home Screen Layout.

Using Multitouch Gestures

As with all iOS apps, you interact with Excel by using your fingertips to perform the **multitouch gestures**, or simply **gestures**, described in Table 1.1.

The iPad's **capacitive** screen contains a dense grid of touch sensors that responds to the electrical field of your fingers or a capacitive stylus. The screen won't respond to a traditional stylus (and you can't wear ordinary gloves). Increasing finger pressure on a capacitive screen, as opposed to a resistive screen, won't increase responsiveness.

> **Tips for Multitouch Gestures**
> - The frame surrounding the screen is called the **bezel**. The bezel doesn't respond to gestures; it's just a place to rest your thumbs.
> - Feel free to use two hands. In Excel, for example, you can use both hands to type on any of the onscreen keyboards. Or you can touch and hold a shape with the finger of one hand, and then use your other hand to tap other shapes to select them all as a group.
> - If you're having trouble with a gesture, make sure that you're not touching the screen's edge with a stray thumb or finger (of either hand).

Table 1.1 Multitouch Gestures

To	Do This
Tap	Gently tap the screen with one finger.
Double-tap	Tap twice quickly. (If you tap too slowly, your iPad interprets it as two single taps.)
Touch and hold	Touch the screen with your finger, and maintain contact with the glass (typically, until some onscreen action happens).
Drag	Touch and hold a point on the screen and then slide your finger across the glass to a different part of the screen. A drag-like **slide** moves a control along a constrained path. You slide the iPad's brightness and volume sliders, for example.
Flick (or swipe)	Fluidly and decisively whip your finger across the screen. A faster flick scrolls the screen faster.
Pinch	Touch your thumb and index finger to the screen and then pinch them together (to zoom out) or spread them apart (to zoom in).
Rotate	Spread your thumb and index finger, touch them to the screen, and then rotate them clockwise or counterclockwise. (Or keep your fingers steady and rotate the iPad itself.)

Figure 1.3 Excel in the App Store search results.

Getting Excel

 You can download Excel from Apple's App Store, available on the iPad itself or from iTunes on your Mac or Windows PC. To use the App Store, your iPad must be connected to the internet and you must have an Apple ID (*appleid.apple.com*).

Tip: To sign in to, change, or create an Apple ID on your iPad, tap Settings > iTunes & App Store.

You can get Excel from the iTunes App Store on your computer and then sync your iPad, but it's simpler and faster to download Excel directly on your iPad. Tap the App Store icon on the Home screen, search for *excel* (or *microsoft office*), find Excel in the search results, and then download it (Figure 1.3). Excel for iPad requires iOS 8.0 or higher.

While you're in the App Store, also download Microsoft's OneDrive app, which you can use to manage Excel files that are stored in the cloud.

Tip: Deleting the Excel app also deletes any workbook files that you've stored locally on your iPad. Workbooks that you've stored in the cloud on OneDrive, Dropbox, or iCloud Drive aren't deleted or changed.

Working with Excel

Excel for iPad lacks some significant features found in its desktop counterparts on Windows and Mac, but it provides a clean workspace suitable for tap-and-drag rather than point-and-click. This section provides an overview of the Excel interface.

Table 1.2 isn't comprehensive, but it will give you an idea of how Excel for iPad compares with Excel for Windows.

Signing in

To use Excel's core features—creating and editing workbooks, storing files in the cloud, collaborating and sharing with others—you must sign in to Excel. The set of core features is extensive and may be all you need, but if you want to unlock Excel completely to use its premium features, then you must sign in with an account that's linked to a qualifying Office 365 subscription:

- **Microsoft account.** If you sign in with a Microsoft account and don't have an Office 365 subscription, you can use Excel's core features for free but must buy a subscription to use premium features. You can create a Microsoft account (using any email address) within Excel for iPad or at *signup.live.com*.

- **Office 365 account.** Sign in with an Office 365 account provided by your organization (work or school). These accounts are volume-purchased multi-user subscriptions that unlock all Excel for iPad features—you don't have to buy your own personal Office 365 subscription.

You can sign in when you first open Excel or, if you tap Sign In Later, when you're already working in Excel. After you sign in, your cloud storage locations appear in backstage view.

Tip: Signing in or out of any Office app (Excel, Word, or PowerPoint) will sign you in or out of them all.

Table 1.2 Selected Features Missing from Excel for iPad

Feature	Feature Actions in Excel for iPad
File viewing	Split and multiple windows aren't supported. Only one view mode is available. Zoom level on open is fixed at 150%.
Data sorting and filtering	Slicers and timelines aren't supported.
Conditional formatting	Viewing is supported. Adding and updating aren't supported.
Data validation	Viewing is supported. Adding and updating aren't supported.
PivotTables	Viewing, refreshing, and adding are supported. Sorting and filtering aren't supported.
Macros	Running macros isn't supported.
External data	Updating files isn't supported.

Figure 1.4 The opening Sign In window.

Figure 1.5 The Sign In window within Excel.

To open Excel and sign in:

1. Do any of the following:
   - Tap the Excel icon on your Home screen.
   - Flick down on your Home screen to reveal the search field, start typing *excel*, and then tap Excel when it appears in the results list.
   - Hold down the Home button until a message asks, "What can I help you with?" Then say "Open Excel".

2. If you previously signed in or tapped Sign In Later, Excel opens to where you last left off; otherwise, sign in to your account (or create a new account) in the Sign In window (Figure 1.4).

   If you're opening Excel for the first time, flick through the introductory windows to reach the Sign In window.

Tip: You can rotate your iPad to use Excel in portrait (tall) or landscape (wide) view.

To sign in within Excel:

1. In backstage view, tap the Sign In icon in the top-left corner.

2. Follow the onscreen instructions.

   After you enter your account credentials (email address and password) and sign in (Figure 1.5), the Sign In icon in backstage view changes to your account icon and shows your name.

Signing out

If you sign out of Excel, you can still access files stored locally on your iPad but not files stored remotely in the cloud. If you're going to lend someone your iPad or travel with it, you can keep your cloud-based files private by bulk-deleting all your sign-in credentials from every Microsoft app on your iPad (Excel, Word, PowerPoint, OneNote, OneDrive, and so on).

To sign out:

- In backstage view, tap your account icon (which may be a personal picture or a generic icon) in the top-left corner, tap your account name, and then tap Sign Out (Figure 1.6).

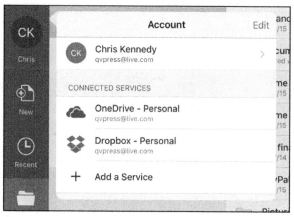

Figure 1.6 The Account menu.

Tip: After you sign out, any pending changes to files stored in the cloud finish syncing in the background.

To delete all your sign-in credentials from all your Microsoft apps:

1. On your iPad's Home screen, tap Settings.
2. On the left side of the Settings screen, scroll down and then tap Excel.
3. On the right side of the Settings screen, tap Reset Excel, and then turn on Delete Login Credentials.
4. Force-close all Microsoft apps: on your iPad, press the Home button twice to show all the apps that are currently open, flick left or right to find a target app, and then flick the app preview up to close it.

If You Don't Sign In

If you don't sign in to a Microsoft account, Excel works as only a simple, read-only file viewer. Without signing in, you can only open and read a workbook that's stored locally on your iPad or located at a SharePoint URL. (**SharePoint** is a set of Microsoft services that large organizations use to manage documents and data.) Excel for iPad displays workbooks—including those created in Excel for Windows or Mac—with near-perfect fidelity. The iPad's built-in file viewer (called Quick Look) and Apple's Numbers app can also display Excel workbooks, though typically with formatting errors and other digital debris.

Tip: If a workbook uses fonts that aren't Office Compatible Fonts or iOS Fonts, then Excel for iPad uses a substitute display font (usually Helvetica) but doesn't change cell formatting.

Backstage view

The file-management hub in Excel is **backstage view** (Figure 1.7), where you can:

- Sign in or out of your Microsoft account
- View lists of your files
- Manage cloud services
- Create, open, share, or delete workbooks
- View workbook properties
- Subscribe to Office 365

To open backstage view:

- If you're opening Excel for the first time, flick through the introductory windows (and optionally sign in) to open backstage view.

  or

  If you don't see backstage view, it means a workbook is already open; tap ⊖ in the top-left corner of the screen.

Tip: Office apps are color-coded so that you'll always know which app you're using when switching among them: Excel = green, Word = blue, and PowerPoint = orange.

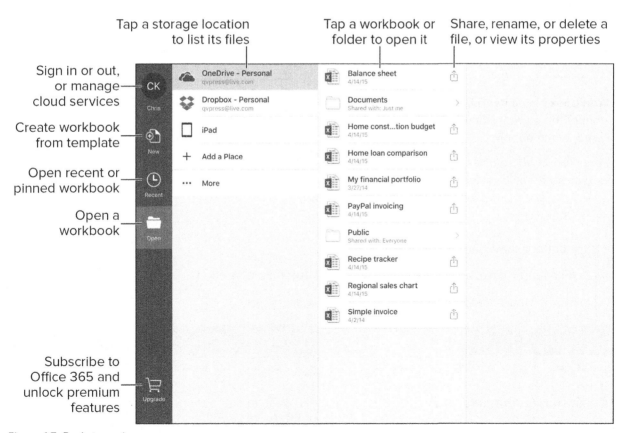

Figure 1.7 Backstage view.

The ribbon

After you create a new workbook or tap an existing one in backstage view, Excel opens that workbook for you to view or edit. Workbooks share a set of controls in the **ribbon** at the top of the screen (Figure 1.8).

Back button. Tap ⬅ to return to backstage view. If AutoSave is turned off, Excel prompts you to save your changes.

File menu. Tap 🗐 or 🗋 to open the File menu (Figure 1.9). You can toggle AutoSave, name a new workbook, duplicate or print a workbook, and more. For details, see "Workbooks" on page 31 and "Printing Files" on page 26.

Undo/Redo. Excel stores your actions, so you can undo and redo them. To undo your last change, tap ↶. To redo the last change that you undid, tap ↷. To undo or redo many changes, tap the buttons repeatedly.

Tip: You can also view or restore previous versions of a workbook (page 36).

Workbook file name. The file name (without extension) of the current workbook appears in the top-center of the ribbon.

Find. Tap 🔍 to search the current workbook or worksheet for all instances of a particular word or

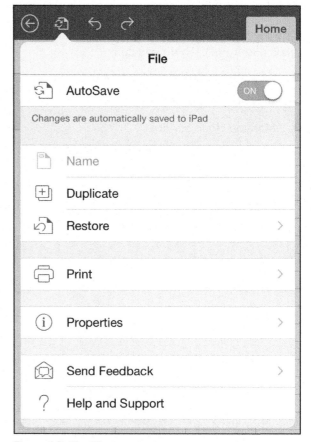

Figure 1.9 The File menu.

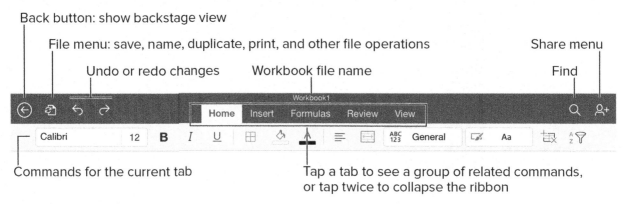

Figure 1.8 The Excel ribbon.

12   Excel for iPad & iPad Pro

Figure 1.10 The Share menu.

phrase, and optionally replace each occurrence with new text. For details, see "Using Editing Tools" on page 57.

Share menu. Tap ♀+ to share the current workbook as a web link or as an email attachment in Excel or PDF format (Figure 1.10).

Ribbon tabs. Almost everything you'll want to do in Excel—from changing background colors to building formulas—is packed into the ribbon. To accommodate all these commands in a compact space, the ribbon uses **tabs**. When you tap a tab, you see a new collection of commands.

The ribbon makes it easy to find features because Excel groups related commands under the same tab. You can also use the ribbon to explore Excel: after you find the command you need, look for other, associated commands on the same tab.

Throughout this book, you'll use the ribbon's tabs to find important features. Here's a quick overview of what each tab provides:

- **Home.** You'll probably spend most of your time with the Home tab selected. This tab contains formatting commands, style commands, commands to insert or delete rows or columns, and commands to sort or filter data.

- **Insert.** Use this tab to add tables and objects to a worksheet. **Objects** are design elements that you drag across a worksheet's canvas to create a layout. Excel objects include charts, pictures, shapes, text boxes, and add-ins, which you can select, move, resize, rotate, copy, delete, layer, style, and manipulate by using the same basic techniques common to all Office apps.

- **Formulas.** This tab helps you build formulas. You can also use it to AutoSum a range or recalculate a workbook.

- **Review.** Add, edit, view, or delete workbook comments.

- **View.** Use this tab to switch on and off various viewing options.

In addition to the standard tabs, Excel includes **contextual tabs**. When a table, pivot table, or object (chart, picture, shape, text box, or add-in) is selected, the ribbon sprouts a special tab for working with that object. Figure 1.11 shows the contextual tab that appears when a chart is selected. When a contextual tab appears, you can continue to use all the other tabs.

If you want to devote more screen space to your workbook, you can **collapse** the ribbon to a single row of tab titles: tap the active tab or double-tap any tab. To return the ribbon to its normal state, tap any tab. Figure 1.12 shows a collapsed ribbon.

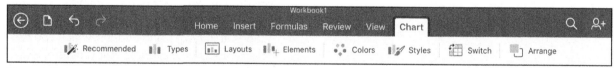

Figure 1.11 Contextual tabs appear and disappear depending on the selection. The Chart tab, for example, appears only when a chart is selected

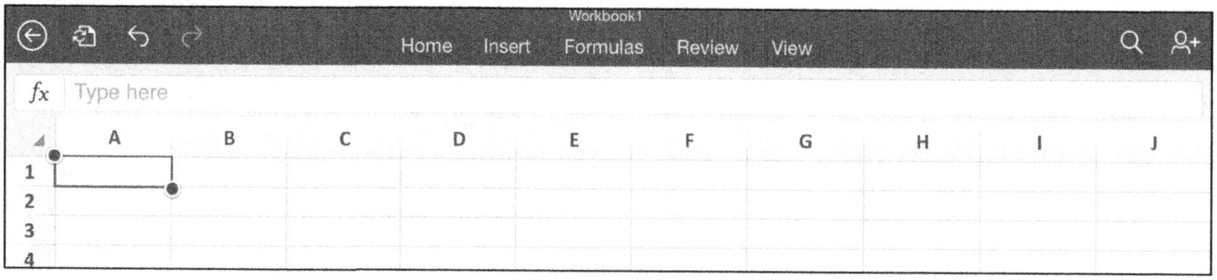

Figure 1.12 A collapsed ribbon occupies less screen space.

CHAPTER 2

Storing, Sharing, and Printing Files

This chapter explains how to:

- Store your files locally on your iPad or in the cloud on OneDrive, Dropbox, or iCloud Drive
- Work offline
- Resolve editing conflicts
- Share your files with others in Excel or PDF format
- Print your files

Tip: For a list of file types that Excel for iPad can work with, see "Supported File Types" on page 30.

Local Storage on Your iPad

File storage on an iPad isn't as simple as it is on Macs and Windows PCs because the iPad has no centralized file storage area. You can't use drag-and-drop to transfer files directly between your iPad and computer, or open documents already on your iPad in any app you choose. Instead, each iPad app keeps its data in a sandbox: a private storage area that other apps can't see or change.

If your needs are simple, you can store your workbook files locally on your iPad: when you first save or duplicate a workbook, choose ☐ iPad as the storage location (Figure 2.1). You can't create folders; you just get "iPad". With local storage, files open and save quickly, an internet connection isn't needed, and your files remain private, but you lose the sharing and syncing benefits of cloud storage.

Tip: To move a local file to cloud storage, or vice versa, see "Copying, moving, and deleting workbooks" on page 35.

Transferring files between your iPad and computer

You can use iTunes on your Mac or Windows PC to:

- Copy Excel workbooks created on your iPad to make them available in iTunes (to, say, copy to your computer's hard drive and print or back up).

- Add workbooks from your computer to a special place in iTunes to copy them to Excel on your iPad over a USB connection.

Using iTunes to transfer document files isn't like syncing photos, videos, music, and apps between your computer and your iPad. iTunes doesn't sync documents; it copies them. Every copy operation to or from your iPad is a manual, one-way process—copies exist independently of one another. For example, if you create an Excel workbook on your iPad and then copy it to your computer, any changes that you make in either copy won't replace or update the other.

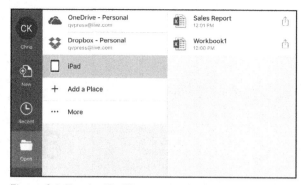

Figure 2.1 Tap the iPad location to show locally stored files.

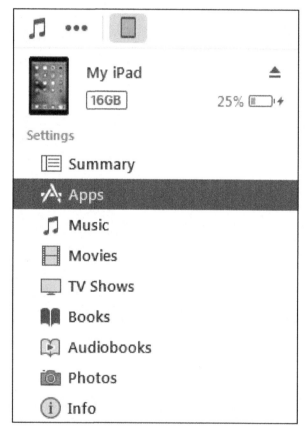

Figure 2.2 Select your iPad in the iTunes sidebar or toolbar.

To copy an Excel workbook from your iPad to your computer:

1. Connect your iPad to your computer via a USB cable and then open iTunes on your computer.

2. In the iTunes sidebar or toolbar, click the icon for your iPad.

   If your iPad doesn't appear in iTunes, make sure that your iPad is unlocked.

3. In the iTunes sidebar, click Apps under Settings, and then scroll to the File Sharing section at the bottom of the window (Figure 2.2).

4. In the Apps list under File Sharing, click Excel.

5. In the Excel Documents list (Figure 2.3), select the workbook(s) that you want to copy to your computer. You can Control-click (or Command-click on the Mac) to select or deselect individual items, or Shift-click to select a contiguous range of items.

6. Drag the workbook(s) from the Excel Documents list to your desktop or another folder on your computer.

   or

   Click Save To, navigate to the destination folder, and then click Choose (or Select Folder).

   iTunes copies the workbook(s) to your computer.

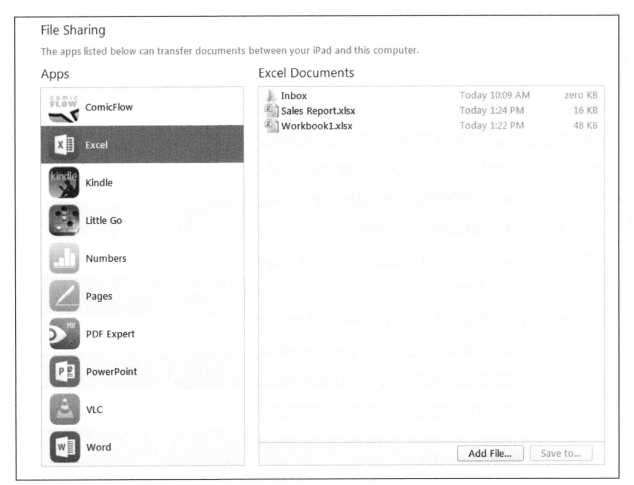

Figure 2.3 The Excel Documents list in iTunes.

To copy an Excel workbook from your computer to your iPad:

1. Connect your iPad to your computer via a USB cable and then open iTunes on your computer.

2. In the iTunes sidebar or toolbar, click the icon for your iPad.

   If your iPad doesn't appear in iTunes, make sure that your iPad is unlocked.

3. In the iTunes sidebar, click Apps under Settings, and then scroll to the File Sharing section at the bottom of the window.

4. In the Apps list under File Sharing, click Excel.

5. Click Add, locate and select the workbook(s) that you want to import, and then click Choose (or Open).

   or

   Drag the workbook(s) that you want to copy to your iPad from your desktop or from a folder window to the Excel Documents list.

6. On your iPad, open Excel.

   The copied files appear in the ☐ iPad location in backstage view.

iTunes backs up your iPad automatically each time that you sync. These backups include files within Excel. If you restore from one of these backups, your Excel for iPad files will be restored. If you don't sync (that is, if you manage your iPad's content manually), then keep backup copies of your Excel files in a dedicated folder outside of iTunes.

Cloud Storage on OneDrive

OneDrive is a **cloud** (online) storage and computing service that uploads (copies) your files to Microsoft's remote data center and pushes them wirelessly to your devices, including Windows PCs, Macs, tablets, and smartphones. OneDrive stores your files and keeps them up to date across all your devices, so that you always have the most current versions at hand, no matter which device you used to make your latest edits. After you sign in and connect to a OneDrive service, every time that you edit a cloud-based workbook in Excel for iPad, your changes are available automatically on all your devices, provided you're connected to the same OneDrive service on each device.

When you create a Microsoft account, you get 5 GB of free OneDrive storage space. If that's not enough, you can buy more for an annual fee: go to *onedrive.com* and then tap or click Plans at the top of the page.

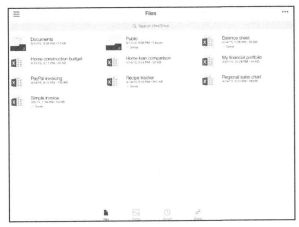

Figure 2.4 The OneDrive app running on an iPad.

Tip: OneDrive used to be called **SkyDrive**. You'll sometimes still see *SkyDrive* used in documentation, online forums, and web addresses.

The OneDrive app and OneDrive.com

 Excel for iPad supports only a few basic file-management operations for files stored on OneDrive—you can share, duplicate, and delete workbooks, for example—but to organize files in folders, manage files in bulk, change settings, or check your storage space, you must sign in to OneDrive in a browser at *onedrive.com* or use Microsoft's free **OneDrive app**, which is available for Android, iOS (Apple iDevices), Windows Vista or later (not XP), Windows Phone, Xbox 360, and Xbox One. Figure 2.4 shows the OneDrive app for the iPad, which you can download from the App Store.

Other Supported Cloud Services

In addition to OneDrive, Excel for iPad supports the following cloud services:

- **Dropbox.** To connect to your Dropbox account from Excel, in backstage view, tap Add a Place, and then tap Dropbox. You can manage Dropbox storage at *dropbox.com* or by using the free Dropbox app (which you can download from the App Store).

- **iCloud Drive.** To connect to your iCloud Drive from Excel, in backstage view, tap More. To enable iCloud Drive, on your iPad's Home screen, tap Settings, tap iCloud (on the left side of the Settings screen), tap iCloud Drive (on the right side of the Settings screen), and then turn on both iCloud Drive and Excel. You can manage iCloud Drive storage at *icloud.com* or by using the Settings app.

Connecting to OneDrive

Signing in to Excel for iPad connects your account's OneDrive service automatically. To manage OneDrive services, tap your account icon in backstage view to open the Account menu (Figure 2.5).

- To add other OneDrive services (say, for separate home and work accounts or different family members), tap Add a Service on the Account menu.

- When you're disconnected from a service that you previously added, a warning icon ⚠ appears next to that service's name on the Account menu.

- To remove a service, tap Edit on the Account menu and then tap the remove icon ⊖ next to the target service.

- You can't remove the OneDrive service for the account that you're signed in to (without signing out).

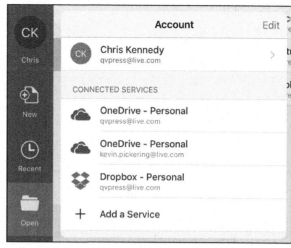

Figure 2.5 The Account menu lists connected cloud services Share menu.

> ### OneDrive for Business
> Some organizations provide their users with **OneDrive for Business** services for large-scale document storage, collaboration, and user-management.
>
> - OneDrive for Business is different from OneDrive, which is intended for personal storage separate from your workplace.
>
> - Files that you place in OneDrive for Business are private by default, unless you place them in the Shared with Everyone folder.
>
> - OneDrive for Business offers enterprise features such as centralized administration and access to an organization's address book.
>
> - OneDrive for Business is also different from yet another type of storage called **team sites**. Team site libraries store team or project-related files that need site-based or granular ownership and permissions across a wide collection of people. Generally, files shared on OneDrive for Business should have a limited scope or lifetime (a blog article that you'd like a few colleagues to review or edit before you post it, for example).

> ### Excel Online
> You can also create and edit cloud-based Excel workbooks in a web browser by using the **Excel Online** web app at *office.live.com*. Workbooks created using Excel Online are automatically available across your devices—and vice versa: if you create a workbook by using Excel on a device, it appears automatically on the web in Excel Online.

Figure 2.6 To change the file, tap Edit on the Offline Copy message bar.

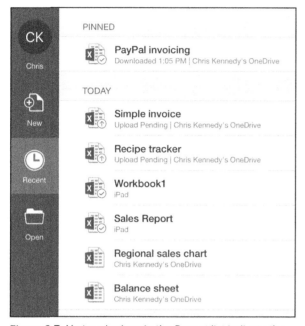

Figure 2.7 Various badges in the Recent list indicate the cache and sync status of files.

Working Offline

If you've used Excel 2013 or later for Windows, you know that when you open a OneDrive-based workbook in Excel, that workbook is synced to your local PC and becomes available while you're **offline** (not connected to the internet). Despite being designed to work on limited-storage tablets, Excel for iPad works similarly. When you open a OneDrive-based workbook in Excel for iPad, you open it from the cloud, make changes, and then save it again back to the cloud. But the workbook is also retained, or **cached**, on your iPad, so you can still open and edit it normally even when you're offline—on an airplane or at a beach, for example. A cached document has a checkmark badge ⊘ on its icon in the Recent list in backstage view.

Tip: Locally stored workbooks always have a checkmark badge ⊘ on their icons.

When you first open a cached workbook while offline, a "[Read-Only]" label appears next to the file name in the ribbon and an Offline Copy message bar appears below the ribbon. To change the file, tap Edit on the message bar (Figure 2.6).

If you edit a cached workbook while offline, Excel for iPad will (by default) autosave the changes, and the workbook's icon in backstage view will have a pending badge ⊙ to show that there are changes to upload to the cloud (Figure 2.7). After you connect online, the changes will be synced to OneDrive. A syncing badge ⟳ appears on the workbook's icon while changes are being uploaded. After syncing completes, the badge changes to a checkmark ⊘ . For small workbooks, syncing takes only a few seconds.

Tip: By default, Excel autosaves your edits as you work. To save changes manually, open any workbook, tap the File icon ⎙, and then turn off AutoSave. The File icon changes to ⎗. To save manually, tap ⎗ and then tap Save. Or tap ⎌ to be prompted to save changes.

Caching and uncaching workbooks

An uncached workbook, which can't be opened when you're offline, has no badge on its icon in backstage view. To cache a workbook manually on your iPad before you fly (or whatever), simply open it and then close it (you don't have to make or save any changes). To make sure that a workbook is cached, confirm that its icon has a checkmark badge ⊘ in the Recent list in backstage view.

You can't uncache workbooks individually, but you can uncache them all. The following procedure clears the iPad cache of *all* Office files, including all Excel workbooks, Word documents, and PowerPoint presentations. Don't clear the cache if any files have pending changes ⊕ or are syncing ⊚.

To uncache all Office documents:

1   On your iPad's Home screen, tap Settings.

2   On the left side of the Settings screen, scroll down and then tap Excel.

3   On the right side of the Settings screen, tap Reset Excel, and then turn on Clear All Workbooks.

4   Force-close all Microsoft apps: on your iPad, press the Home button twice to show all the apps that are currently open, flick left or right to find a target app, and then flick the app preview up to close it.

Note that you can tap ☆ to **pin** often-needed workbooks so that they always appear at the top of the Recent list in backstage view. Pinning is only a convenience, and pinned workbooks are treated no differently from other workbooks with regard to caching. To use pinned workbooks offline, you must still cache them manually by opening and then closing them.

Figure 2.8 To resolve an editing conflict, tap Resolve on the Cannot Save message bar.

Resolving Editing Conflicts

An **editing conflict** occurs if a cloud-based workbook is edited on two devices before being updated on either device. For example, if you edit a workbook on your iPad and someone else edits the same workbook on a different iPad before your changes are synced (pushed) from your iPad to the cloud, then the last person to save will get an editing conflict. Editing conflicts typically occur when collaborators edit the same workbook while offline, but you can cause a conflict by yourself if you edit the same workbook across multiple devices.

When a conflict occurs, a Cannot Save message bar appears below the ribbon. To resolve the conflict, tap Resolve on the message bar (Figure 2.8).

You can either duplicate the workbook (that is, create another version with a different name) or throw away all your changes. Unfortunately, you can't merge everyone's changes into the same workbook (Figure 2.9).

Neither resolution is satisfying. If you discard your changes, you lose your recent edits permanently. If you duplicate, you end up with two workbooks: one with your changes, and another with the other person's changes. If you are working on a large workbook or have made many changes, then you've got a problem. The moral: make the consequences of conflicts clear to all your collaborators and schedule edits accordingly. If you work alone on multiple devices, don't work offline on one device without first syncing any changes made on the other devices.

Tip: The Duplicate command is equivalent to the Save As command in Excel for Windows.

In backstage view, workbooks with editing conflicts are marked with a warning icon ⚠. Tap the icon to resolve the conflict (Figure 2.10).

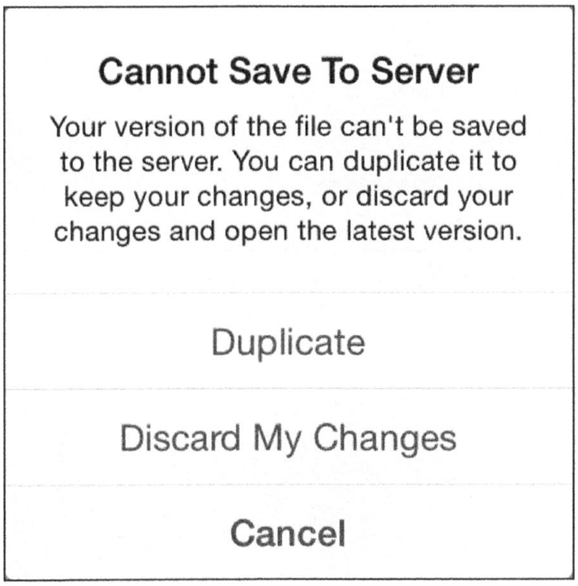

Figure 2.9 Two resolutions are available: duplicate the workbook or throw away all your changes.

Figure 2.10 In backstage view, warning icons flag editing conflicts.

Chapter 2 Storing, Sharing, and Printing Files 23

Sharing Files

You can send copies of files in Excel or PDF format from your iPad via email. If a file is saved in the cloud, then you can send links instead of copies. You can also save and open files that you receive on your iPad.

Tip: A link is a URL (web address) that the recipient can tap or click to view the file. The best way to share a file is to put it on OneDrive and send others a link to it. This way, you can make changes whenever you want and the people you shared the link with always have the latest version.

Figure 2.11 The Share menu.

To share a file from your iPad:

1. On your iPad, open Excel.
2. If you're in backstage view, tap 📤 next to the name of the file that you want to share, and then tap Share.

   or

   If you have the file open, tap 👤+ in the ribbon (Figure 2.11).
3. Tap a sharing option:
   - **Invite People.** Send a link via email. Choose whether you want people to be able to only view the file or edit it too. This sharing option isn't available if the file is stored locally on your iPad.
   - **Send Attachment.** Send a copy of the file as an email attachment in Excel or PDF format.

Figure 2.12 An email message with an attached Excel workbook.

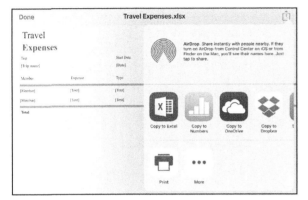

Figure 2.13 The Open In menu lets you open and save files in compatible apps.

▸ **Copy Link.** Copy a link to the clipboard. Choose whether you want people to be able to only view the file or edit it too. You can paste the link in an email, message, note, or social network post to share it with someone. This sharing option isn't available if the file is stored locally on your iPad.

Tip: Links aren't private—anyone who has the link can access the file.

▸ **Shared With.** View or change the editing permissions of people you've shared the file with.

To save a file from an email message to your iPad:

1. On your iPad, open Mail.

2. Open the message containing the attached file (Figure 2.12). Attachments appear as icons in the body of the message. The file size can give you an idea of how long the download will take.

3. If necessary, tap the file's icon to download it. (Some attachments download automatically when you open the message.)

4. When the download completes, tap the file's icon again.

    A preview of the spreadsheet opens in Mail.

5. In the toolbar at the top of the screen, tap ⬆ (Figure 2.13). (If the toolbar disappears, tap anywhere on the screen to bring it back.)

6. Open the file in the desired app (which can be any app that can read or share Excel files, not necessarily Excel itself). The file is saved in the specified app.

Chapter 2 Storing, Sharing, and Printing Files   25

Printing Files

You can print Excel workbooks wirelessly from an **AirPrint**-capable printer that you've set up to work with your iPad. To set up a printer, read the Apple support article "About AirPrint" at *support.apple.com/kb/HT201311*.

To print a workbook from an AirPrint-capable printer:

1. Open the workbook that you want to print.
2. Tap ⤴ or 🗎 and then tap Print.
3. Choose the layout options and then tap Next (Figure 2.14).
4. Choose the printer options and then tap Print.

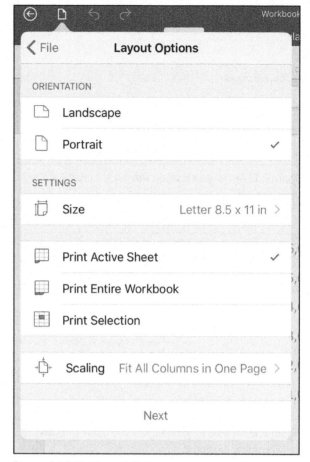

Figure 2.14 The Layout Options menu.

Other Ways to Print

You have other ways to print, with or without AirPrint.

- **Transfer the file to your computer.** Email the workbook or copy it from the cloud to your Mac or Windows PC, open it in Excel, and then print it normally.

- **Use Numbers for iOS.** Numbers, Apple's spreadsheet app, can open Excel workbooks and print them wirelessly via AirPrint. Note that Numbers can't display or print all Excel workbook features with perfect fidelity. If you bought your iPad in September 2013 or later, Numbers is free.

- **Use a print app.** Use a third-party app that provides iPad-based printing by getting a workbook from an app and then sending it to a printer—either directly to a shared network printer or wirelessly via a helper program that you install on your computer. To find a print app, search for *print* or *printer* in the App Store. The app ThinPrint Cloud Printer, for example, lets you print files directly from your iPad: select any Office for iPad file in Microsoft's OneDrive app, tap •••, tap Open in Another App, and then tap ThinPrint. Your file prints immediately.

CHAPTER 3

Spreadsheet Basics

You'll need the skills covered in this chapter to create your spreadsheets (called **workbooks** in Excel-speak), no matter how simple or complex.

The Excel Workspace

Figure 3.1 shows you the important parts of Excel for iPad, which are described in Table 3.1.

The work you do in Excel is performed in a workbook file. You can have only one workbook open at a time. By default, Excel workbooks use a .xlsx filename extension. Each workbook contains one or more worksheets, and each worksheet is made up of a grid of cells. Each cell can contain a value: a number, text, a date, the result of a formula, and so on. A worksheet also has a transparent drawing layer (like a clear acetate overlay), which holds charts, pictures, shapes, text boxes, and add-ins. Each worksheet in a workbook is accessible by tapping its tab at the bottom of the workbook. Think of a worksheet as a flexible, freeform "canvas" where you can enter and organize data; create tables and charts; insert text and graphics; and create formulas with functions and operators.

In addition, a workbook can store chart sheets; a chart sheet displays a single chart and is also accessible by tapping its tab. You can view, but not create, chart sheets in Excel for iPad.

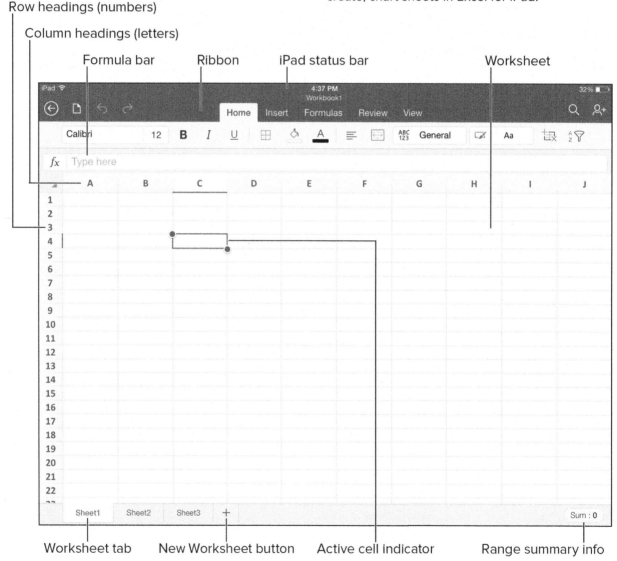

Figure 3.1 The Excel workspace.

28 Excel for iPad & iPad Pro

Table 3.1 The Main Parts of the Excel Workspace

Feature or Control	Description
Row headings	Row headings are numbers that range from 1 to 1,048,576—one for each row in the worksheet. You can tap a row number to select an entire row of cells, or drag a row border to change its height.
Column headings	Column headings are letters that range from A to XFD—one for each of the 16,384 columns in the worksheet. You can tap a column heading to select an entire column of cells, or drag a column border to change its width.
Formula bar	When you enter values or formulas in a cell, it appears in this bar.
Ribbon	The ribbon is the main location for Excel commands. Tapping a tab shows a different set of commands. For details, see "The ribbon" on page 12.
iPad status bar	This narrow strip runs along the top of the Home screen, Lock screen, and many application screens (including Excel). It shows the current time and displays icons that indicate the current state of your iPad, including network connectivity and battery level.
Worksheet	A worksheet is the primary work area in Excel that you use to store, organize, and analyze data. Each worksheet consists of cells that are arranged in a grid of columns and rows.
Worksheet tabs	Each of these notebook-like tabs represents a different worksheet in the workbook. A workbook can have any number of worksheets, and each worksheet's name is displayed on its worksheet tab.
New Worksheet button	Add a new worksheet by tapping the + button to the right of the last worksheet tab.
Active cell indicator	This heavy border indicates the currently active cell (one of the 17,179,869,184 cells on each worksheet).
Range summary info	This self-updating label shows summary statistics about the range of cells selected. Tap the label to change the information displayed (sum, count, average, and so on).

Supported File Types

Excel for iPad doesn't support as many file types as Excel for Windows and Mac do. If you can't open a file, it's probably because it's been saved in a file format that Excel for iPad doesn't support. Check Table 3.2 to see whether that's the case.

Table 3.2 Files That You Can and Can't Open in Excel for iPad

File Type	Compatibility
Excel workbooks (.xlsx and .xls)	Open and edit
Excel templates (.xltx)	Open and edit
Non-XML binary workbooks (.xlsb)	Open and edit
Comma-delimited (.csv)	Open and edit
Macro-enabled workbooks (.xlsm)	Open as read-only (no editing)
Macro and dialog worksheets	Open as read-only (no editing)
IRM-protected files	Not supported
Excel templates (.xlt)	Not supported
Macro-enabled templates (.xltm)	Not supported
Macro-enabled add-ins (.xla and .xlam)	Not supported
Extensible markup language (.xml)	Not supported
Data interchange format (.dif)	Not supported
Hypertext markup language (.htm and .html)	Not supported
Archived webpages (.mht and .mhtml)	Not supported
Printable files (.prn)	Not supported
Symbolic link files (.slk and .sylk)	Not supported
Plain text files (.txt)	Not supported
Binary interchange files (Biff2, Biff3, Biff4, Biff5)	Not supported

Workbooks

To get started with Excel, launch it and then either open an existing workbook or create a new one based on one of the predesigned **templates**. Templates contain ready-made layouts, tables, charts, text boxes, and other elements—they're the quickest way to start a project because much of the work has been done for you. Exploring the different templates can show you how to assemble tables, charts, text, shapes, and pictures into pleasing or professional-looking workbooks.

- Each template is intended for a specific purpose (personal, business, or education). Even if you don't use a template for its intended purpose, you still can choose it for its looks (color scheme, fonts, and formatting) and then delete its contents but not its style.

- To build your workbook from scratch, use the Blank Workbook template.

- Editing a workbook doesn't affect the template on which it's based.

- You can't edit or delete the built-in templates.

- You can download hundreds of other templates from the Microsoft Office website at *templates.office.com*.

Tip: Excel for iPad supports only a few basic file-management operations for files stored on OneDrive—you can share, duplicate, rename, and delete workbooks, for example. But to organize files in folders, manage files in bulk, change settings, or check your storage space, use the OneDrive app or website (page 19).

Creating and opening workbooks

In backstage view, you can create a new workbook or open an existing one from local or cloud storage.

To create a new workbook:

1. In backstage view, tap ⊕ New.

2. In the templates screen, flick up or down to see all the templates. The Blank Workbook template gives you an empty workbook. The other templates contain a mix of sample data, tables, charts, placeholder text, pictures, and shapes.

3. Tap the template that you want to use (Figure 3.2).

   A new workbook opens (Figure 3.3).

To open an existing workbook:

1. In backstage view, do any of the following:

   ▸ To see all your workbooks, tap 📁 Open and then tap a location (Figure 3.4). To list workbooks stored locally on your iPad, tap ⬜ iPad. To list workbooks stored in the cloud, tap OneDrive, Dropbox, or More (for iCloud Drive).

   ▸ To see recently opened and pinned workbooks (local or cloud-based), tap 🕘 Recent (Figure 3.5). Pinned workbooks appear at the top of the Recent list, followed by unpinned workbooks sorted by the time that they were last opened or saved.

Tip: To **pin** an often-needed workbook to the top of the Recent list, tap 📌. To unpin it, tap 📍. To remove a workbook from the Recent list, tap 🗑 and then tap Remove from Recent.

---

2. Tap the workbook that you want to open.

   If necessary, flick up or down the file list or tap a folder. Each list item shows a workbook's file name, location or owner, and modification date.

Tip: To refresh the contents of the Open screen manually, flick or drag down the top of a file list.

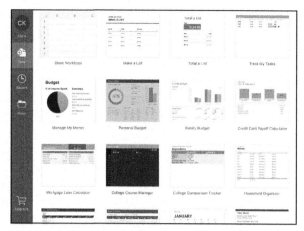

Figure 3.2 Tap a template to create a new workbook.

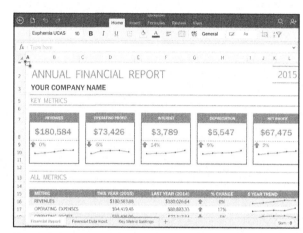

Figure 3.3 A new workbook based on the chosen template.

Figure 3.4 The Open screen.

Figure 3.5 The Recent screen.

Figure 3.6 Toggle AutoSave on the File menu.

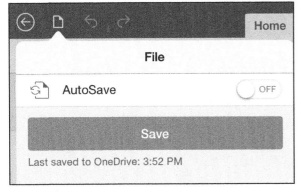

Figure 3.7 Tap Save to save your changes.

Saving and naming workbooks

By default, Excel for iPad saves your changes automatically as you work and when you tap ⊙ to return to backstage view. If you like, you can save changes manually by turning off **AutoSave**. You must name a workbook when you save it the first time.

Tip: If AutoSave is turned on, you can avoid overwriting an original file by creating a copy before you make changes.

To turn AutoSave on or off:

- Open any workbook, tap the File icon ⊡ or ▢ in the ribbon, and then toggle AutoSave (Figure 3.6).

  When AutoSave is turned on, the File icon is ⊡; when it's turned off, the File icon is ▢.

  The AutoSave setting applies to all workbooks.

To save changes manually (AutoSave must be turned off):

- Tap ▢ and then tap Save (Figure 3.7).

  or

  Tap ⊙ to be prompted to save or discard your changes (Figure 3.8).

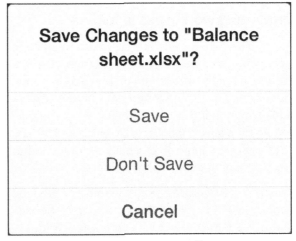

Figure 3.8 When AutoSave is turned off, you can save or discard your changes manually.

Chapter 3 Spreadsheet Basics 33

To name a new workbook:

1. Do any of the following:
   ▸ If AutoSave is turned on, tap ⟲ and then tap Name.
   ▸ If AutoSave is turned off, tap 🗋 and then tap Save.
   ▸ Tap ⟵ and then tap Save.

2. In the Save As window, choose a location, type a file name for the workbook, and then tap Save (Figure 3.9).

   You can double-tap a word to open a pop-up menu of editing commands, or drag across text to move the insertion point.

To rename a workbook:

1. If the workbook is open, tap ⟵ to close it and return to backstage view.

2. Tap 🗀 Open or 🕓 Recent and then locate the workbook that you want to rename.

3. Tap ⬆ and then tap Rename.

Tip: You can also rename a workbook by using the OneDrive app or website (page 19).

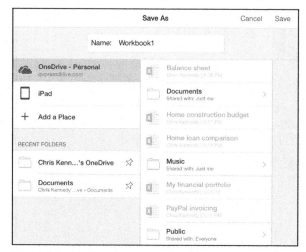

Figure 3.9 Choose a location and type a workbook name in the Save As window.

Organizing workbooks in folders

If too many workbooks are crowding backstage view, you can group them in **folders** to organize them compactly. It's a common practice to create multiple folders, each holding similar types of workbooks (personal, business, projects, travel, and so on). Folders save a lot of screen space and reduce excessive scrolling. You can build a storage hierarchy by creating folders within folders.

You can't use Excel for iPad to create or manage folders. Instead, use the OneDrive app or website (page 19). OneDrive comes with a few folders—Documents, Pictures, and Public—which you can rename, delete, move, and so on. You can't create folders in local storage.

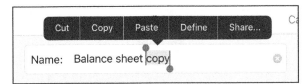

Figure 3.10 Double-tap a word to show a pop-up menu of editing commands.

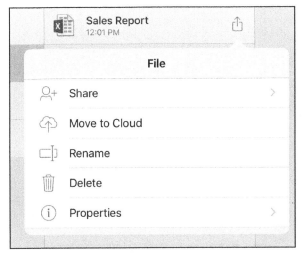

Figure 3.11 The File menu in backstage view.

Copying, moving, and deleting workbooks

You can copy, move, or delete workbooks in Excel for iPad, from local or cloud storage.

To save a copy of a workbook:

1. Open the workbook that you want to copy.
2. Tap 🗐 or 🗋 and then tap Duplicate.
3. Choose a location, type a file name for the new workbook, and then tap Save.

   You can double-tap a word to open a pop-up menu of editing commands (Figure 3.10), or drag across text to move the insertion point.

   After you save, the original workbook closes and the copy remains open.

Tip: The Duplicate command is equivalent to the Save As command in Excel for Windows.

To move a workbook from local storage to cloud storage:

1. If the workbook is open, tap ⬅ to close it and return to backstage view.
2. Tap 📁 Open, tap ☐ iPad, locate the workbook that you want to move, tap ⬆, and then tap Move to Cloud (Figure 3.11).

To copy a workbook from cloud storage to local storage:

1. Open the workbook that you want to copy.
2. Tap 🗐 or 🗋, tap Duplicate, and then save to ☐ iPad.

To delete a workbook:

1. If the workbook is open, tap ⬅ to close it and return to backstage view.
2. Tap 📁 Open and then locate the workbook that you want to delete.
3. Tap ⬆ and then tap Delete (Figure 3.11).

Viewing a workbook's properties and version history

When you or someone else makes changes to a workbook in cloud storage, OneDrive keeps track of the versions automatically, so you don't need to store multiple versions of the same workbook. You can view, restore, or download previous versions of a workbook. Previous versions don't count against your OneDrive storage limit.

How versioning works: OneDrive stores a history of changes (called "deltas" in tech-speak) made to a workbook, and applies those changes in order (or reverse order) to roll forward or back to other versions. If you make a few tiny changes to a 100 MB workbook, for example, OneDrive doesn't store two 100 MB versions. Instead, it stores the current version (100 MB) accompanied by only the changes, which OneDrive can undo to revert to the previous version or redo to restore the current version.

You can also view the properties of the current version of a workbook, including its file name, location, size, modification date, and more.

Tip: Versioning doesn't work for files in local storage.

To view workbook properties:

- In backstage view, tap 📁 Open or 🕒 Recent, tap 📤 next to the workbook of interest, and then tap Properties.

    or

    If the workbook is open, tap 📑 or 📄 and then tap Properties.

    The Properties menu opens (Figure 3.12). (To return to the File menu, tap ❮.)

Tip: To copy property text to the clipboard (for later pasting), touch and hold the text on the Properties menu and then tap Copy on the pop-up menu.

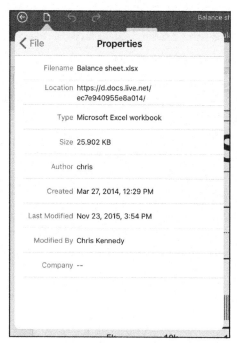

Figure 3.12 The Properties menu.

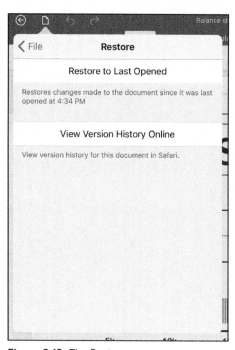

Figure 3.13 The Restore menu.

The Recycle Bin

When you delete a file on OneDrive, it's not actually erased but moved to the **recycle bin**. OneDrive's recycle bin (which works like the recycle bin in Windows and the trash in Mac OS X) is a safeguard from which you can restore (undelete) files to their original locations.

Files in the recycle bin don't count against your OneDrive storage limit, and are stored for a minimum of three days and a maximum of 30 days. The size of the recycle bin is 10% of your storage limit (that's 716 MB for a standard 7 GB OneDrive plan). When the recycle bin runs out of space, OneDrive permanently deletes the oldest files from the recycle bin (provided that they've been in the recycle bin for at least three days) to accommodate newly deleted files.

If you're concerned about privacy or security and don't want your deleted files lingering on OneDrive for up to a month, you can delete them from the recycle bin permanently.

You can't reach the recycle bin from Excel for iPad. Instead, go to *onedrive.com* in a browser, sign in to your Microsoft account, and then tap or click Recycle Bin at the bottom of the left pane. To restore all items, tap or click Restore All Items. To permanently delete all items, tap or click Empty Recycle Bin. To restore or permanently delete individual items, choose them by selecting their checkboxes.

You can also view and manage the contents of the recycle bin in the OneDrive app: tap the menu icon in the top-left corner, tap the gear icon, tap your OneDrive account name, and then tap View Recycle Bin.

To view, restore, or download previous versions of a workbook:

1. Open the workbook.
2. Tap ⤴ or ▢ and then tap Restore.

   The Restore menu opens (Figure 3.13).

3. To undo all your changes since you last opened the workbook, tap Restore to Last Opened.

   or

   To view, restore, or download previous versions of the workbook, tap View Version History Online. The workbook opens in Excel Online (page 20) in the Safari browser. If necessary, sign in to your OneDrive account. Tap an item in the version history list in the left pane (Figure 3.14).

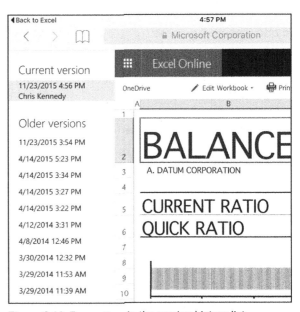

Figure 3.14 Tap an item in the version history list.

Worksheets

Worksheets, or simply **sheets**, are tabs within a workbook that divide information into logical groups. Each new worksheet that you add is ready for data, formulas, tables, charts, pictures, add-ins, and more. For example, you can place a table of raw data on one worksheet and charts, summary statistics, and conclusions on another. Or you can use worksheets to segregate different financial accounts. To get ideas for organizing worksheets, browse the templates (page 31) that came with Excel.

Worksheets are shown as a row of tabs at the bottom of the screen (Figure 3.15). Every new worksheet is given a default name (Sheet1, Sheet2, and so on) that you can change to something more descriptive.

Figure 3.15 A row of worksheet tabs in the tab bar.

Figure 3.16 A colored tab indicates the active worksheet.

Figure 3.17 Double-tap a tab to rename a worksheet.

Tip: To show or hide the worksheet tabs, tap View tab > Sheet Tabs.

To add a new worksheet:

- Tap + to the right of the last worksheet tab.

    You can add as many worksheets as you want to a workbook.

To move from worksheet to worksheet:

- Flick or drag left or right to scroll the tabs along the bottom of the screen, and then tap a tab to activate its worksheet.

    A bright-colored tab indicates the **active** (frontmost) worksheet (Figure 3.16).

To rename a worksheet:

- Double-tap the active worksheet's tab and then type a new name.

    You can double-tap a word to open a pop-up menu of editing commands (Figure 3.17), or drag across text to move the insertion point.

    Worksheets within the same workbook all must have different names. Excel will prevent you from entering a duplicate name.

Figure 3.18 Drag worksheet tabs to reorder them.

Figure 3.19 Tap a tab to open the worksheet menu.

Figure 3.20 The copy appears next to the original worksheet.

To reorder worksheets:

- Touch and hold a worksheet's tab until its color fades slightly, and then drag it left or right to a new position in the tab bar (Figure 3.18).

  The other tabs slide to make way for the one you're dragging. If you want to move a worksheet to a position that's not currently visible, drag its tab off the left or right edge of the tab bar to autoscroll the tabs.

  If you're moving a worksheet a short distance, you can hold-and-flick (rather than hold-and-drag) its tab.

Tip: You can't move a worksheet while you're renaming it (that is, while the insertion point is blinking within the tab's text). Tap outside the text.

To delete a worksheet:

1. Tap the worksheet's tab to activate it.
2. Tap the tab again, and then tap Delete on the pop-up menu (Figure 3.19).

   If the deleted worksheet contains data that are displayed as a chart in another worksheet, then the links are severed and the chart reverts to a placeholder.

Tip: You can't delete the last worksheet in a workbook.

To make a copy of a worksheet:

1. Tap the worksheet's tab to activate it.
2. Tap the tab again, and then tap Duplicate on the pop-up menu.

   The copy appears alongside the original, with a slightly different name (Figure 3.20).

To hide a worksheet:

1 Tap the worksheet's tab to activate it.

2 Tap the tab again, and then tap Hide on the pop-up menu.

   The worksheet is removed from view (Figure 3.21).

Figure 3.21 A hidden worksheet is removed from view.

Tip: The data in hidden worksheets isn't visible, but it can still be referenced from other worksheets.

To unhide a worksheet:

1 Tap the active worksheet's tab (or tap any worksheet tab twice, slowly).

2 Tap Unhide on the pop-up menu and then tap the name of the worksheet to unhide.

Tip: The Unhide command appears on the pop-up menu only if at least one worksheet is hidden.

To zoom in or out on a worksheet:

1 Tap the worksheet's tab to activate it.

2 Touch two fingers to the worksheet and then spread them apart (to zoom in) or pinch them together (to zoom out).

   As you zoom, a pop-up indicator shows the current magnification level, which ranges from 75% to 300%. Zooming is continuous but snaps into place at the 100%, 125%, 150%, and 200% levels.

Tip: By default, Excel zooms to the 150% level when you open a workbook.

Cells, Rows, and Columns

The worksheet grid of **rows** and **columns** is where you organize, analyze, and present data. At each row–column intersection is a **cell**, which can show a value: a number, text, a date, the result of a formula, and so on. (A cell with no contents is called an **empty cell** or **blank cell**.)

Each cell is identified uniquely by its cell reference: an address named for the column letter and row number where the cell is located. Cell B2, for example, is the cell at the intersection of column B and row 2. For details, see "Cell References" on page 79.

Drag or flick a worksheet to scroll it. Each worksheet has 1,048,576 (2^{20}) rows and 16,384 (2^{14}) columns, or about 17.1 (2^{34}) billion cells. Cell A1 is in the top-left corner, and cell XFD1048576 is in the bottom-right corner.

Tip: To show or hide worksheet gridlines, tap View tab > Gridlines.

Selecting cells

The **active cell** is the selected cell in which data is entered when you type or paste. Only one cell is active at a time, and is bounded by a heavy border called the **active cell indicator**.

Tip: To edit the contents of cells, see Chapter 4.

To select a cell:

- Tap the cell.

    A heavy border with selection handles ● surrounds a selected cell (Figure 3.22). (Selection handles won't appear when the onscreen keyboard is open. Tap on the keyboard to dismiss the keyboard.)

To select a range of cells:

1. Tap any cell in the range.

2. Drag the selection handles ● in any direction (up, down, left, right, or diagonally) to encompass the cells that you want to select (Figure 3.23).

    You can release the selection handles and then drag them again to change the selected range. Dragging a selection handle near the edge of the screen autoscrolls the selection in the direction of the drag.

To select all cells in a worksheet:

- Tap the Select All button ◢ in the top-left corner of the worksheet grid (Figure 3.24).

To select a region of cells by flicking:

1. Tap any cell in the region.

2. Flick a selection handle ● in any direction to automatically select all data in that row or column for a contiguous area of the worksheet. This method is especially useful for quickly selecting table data (Chapter 6).

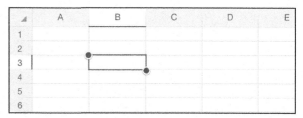

Figure 3.22 A selected cell.

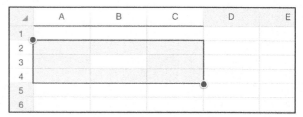

Figure 3.23 A range of selected cells.

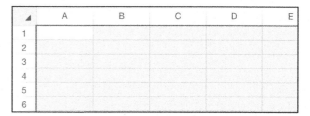

Figure 3.24 A worksheet with all cells selected.

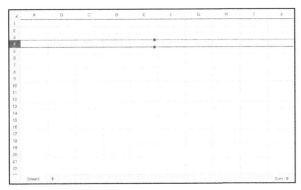

Figure 3.25 A selected row.

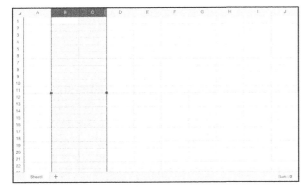

Figure 3.26 Selected columns.

Selecting rows and columns

When you select a row or column, you can manage masses of data easily—move or copy the selection to a new location in the worksheet, delete the entire row or column, format all the cells in the selection, and more.

Tip: When you select columns or rows, a pop-up menu appears next to the selection. You can summon or dismiss this menu by tapping the selection's row or column heading.

To select entire rows or columns:

1. To select an entire row, tap the numbered heading on the left edge of the row (Figure 3.25). To select the fourth row, for example, tap the "4" box to the left of the row. Excel highlights all the columns in row 4.

   or

   To select an entire column, tap the lettered heading at the top of the column. To select the second column, for example, tap the "B" box above the column. Excel selects all the cells in the column, down to row 1,048,576.

2. To extend the selection, drag the selection handles ● to encompass the rows or columns that you want to select (Figure 3.26).

Chapter 3 Spreadsheet Basics 43

Inserting and deleting cells, rows, and columns

You can insert blank cells above or to the left of the active cell in a worksheet. When you insert blank cells, Excel shifts other cells in the same column down or cells in the same row to the right to accommodate the new cells. Similarly, you can insert rows above a selected row and columns to the left of a selected column. You can also delete cells, rows, and columns.

The Insert & Delete Cells menu holds insert and delete commands for cells, rows, and columns. To open it, tap the Home tab and then tap 🗗 (Figure 3.27).

Insertions and deletions affect formulas. When you insert cells, all references that are affected by the insertion adjust accordingly, whether they are relative or absolute cell references. The same behavior applies to deleting cells, except when a deleted cell is directly referenced by a formula. If you want references to adjust automatically, it's a good idea to use range references (when appropriate) in your formulas, instead of specifying individual cells. For details, see Chapter 5.

To insert cells:

1. Select the cell or the range of cells where you want to insert the new blank cells. Select the same number of cells that you want to insert. To insert four blank cells, for example, you must select four cells.

2. On the Home tab, tap 🗗 and then tap Shift Cells Down or Shift Cells Right.

To insert rows:

1. To insert a single row, select either the entire row or a cell in the row above which you want to insert the new row. To insert a new row above row 4, for example, select row 4 or tap any cell in row 4.

    or

    To insert multiple rows, select either the entire rows or cells in the rows above which you want to insert rows. Select the same number of rows that you want to insert. To insert three new rows, for example, you must select three rows.

2. On the Home tab, tap 🗗 and then tap Insert Sheet Rows.

    or

    Tap Insert Above on the pop-up menu (Figure 3.28). (This command appears only when entire rows are selected.)

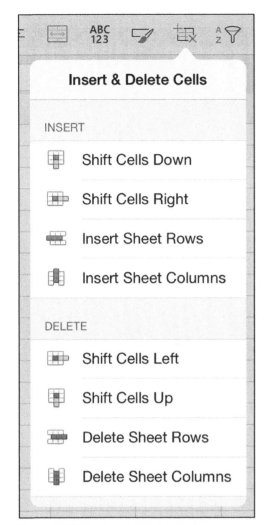

Figure 3.27 The Insert & Delete Cells menu.

Figure 3.28 Tap Insert Above to insert a row.

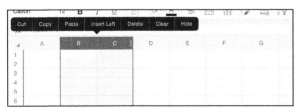

Figure 3.29 Tap Insert Left to insert columns.

To insert columns:

1. To insert a single column, select either the entire column or a cell in the column to the right of where you want to insert the new column. To insert a new column to the left of column B, for example, select column B or tap any cell in column B.

   or

   To insert multiple columns, select either the entire columns or cells in the columns to the right of where you want to insert columns. Select the same number of columns that you want to insert. To insert three new columns, for example, you must select three columns.

2. On the Home tab, tap ⊞ and then tap Insert Sheet Columns.

   or

   Tap Insert Left on the pop-up menu (Figure 3.29). (This command appears only when entire columns are selected.)

To delete cells, rows, or columns:

1. Select the cells, rows, or columns that you want to delete.

2. On the Home tab, tap ⊞ and then tap one of the Delete commands: Shift Cells Left, Shift Cells Up, Delete Sheet Rows, or Delete Sheet Columns.

   or

   Tap Delete on the pop-up menu. (This command appears only when entire rows or columns are selected.)

   If you delete a cell or a range of cells, then cells shift left or up depending on which command you choose. If you delete entire rows or columns, then other rows or columns shift left or up automatically.

Tip: Excel keeps formulas up to date by adjusting references to the shifted cells to reflect their new locations. A formula that refers to a deleted cell, however, displays the #REF! error value.

Chapter 3 Spreadsheet Basics 45

Moving and copying rows and columns

You can use the cut, copy, and paste commands to move or copy selected rows and columns, or move rows or columns quickly by dragging them. When you move or copy rows and columns, Excel moves or copies all the data that they contain, including formulas and their resulting values, comments, cell formats, and hidden cells. See also "Cutting, Copying, and Pasting Cells" on page 64.

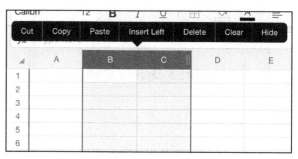

Figure 3.30 The pop-up menu for selected columns.

To move or copy rows or columns:

1. Select the rows or columns that you want to move or copy.

2. To move rows or columns, tap Cut on the pop-up menu (Figure 3.30).

   or

   To copy rows or columns, tap Copy on the pop-up menu.

3. Select a row or column below or to the right of where you want to move or copy your selection.

4. Tap Paste on the pop-up menu.

Tip: A dashed border, also called a marquee or "marching ants", surrounds a cut or copied selection. As long as the marquee is present, you can paste the content of the selection elsewhere.

To move rows or columns by dragging:

1. Select the rows or columns that you want to move.

2. Touch and hold the selection until it rises out of the worksheet.

   Touch and hold a selected cell, not the row or column headings.

3. Drag it to another location in the same worksheet.

   A transparent image of the original cells follows your drag. Excel indicates where the selection will land when you lift your finger. (You can't drag to another worksheet.)

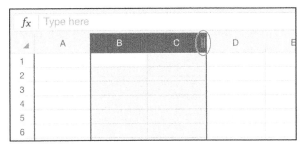

Figure 3.31 Drag the edge of the selection heading to resize columns or rows.

Resizing rows and columns

You can change the height of rows or width of columns manually, or use AutoFit to resize a row or column to fit its content automatically.

To resize a row or column manually:

- To resize a row, touch and hold the bottom edge of the row heading until thin lines appear, and then drag up or down.

    or

    To resize a column, touch and hold the right edge of the column heading until thin lines appear, and then drag left or right.

    The row or column doesn't have to be selected to resize it.

Tip: If the heading edges are too small to touch accurately, zoom in by spreading two fingers on the worksheet.

To resize multiple rows or columns manually:

1. Select the rows or columns that you want to resize.

2. To resize rows, drag the bottom edge of the row heading ▤ up or down.

    or

    To resize columns, drag the right edge of the column heading ▯ left or right (Figure 3.31).

    All the selected rows or columns are resized to the same height or width.

To autofit rows or columns to the size of the tallest or widest entry:

- Select the rows or columns that you want to resize and then tap AutoFit on the pop-up menu. All the selected rows or columns are resized.

    or

    Double-tap a row or column heading.

Freezing rows and columns

Freezing forces a specific set of rows or columns to remain visible at all times. When you freeze data, it remains fixed in place in the Excel window, even as you move to another location in the worksheet. Suppose you want to keep visible the first row in a worksheet because it contains column titles. When you freeze that row, you can always tell what's in each column beneath—even when you scroll far down the worksheet. Similarly, if your first column holds unique identifiers, you can freeze it so that, when you scroll rightward, you don't lose track of the IDs.

You can freeze rows at the top of your worksheet, or columns at the left of your worksheet, with a few limits:

- You can freeze only adjacent rows or columns. You can't freeze columns A and C without freezing column B, for example. (You can, of course, freeze only one row or column.)

- If a row or column isn't visible and you freeze it, you can't see it until you unfreeze it. If you scroll down so that row 100 appears at the top of the worksheet grid, for example, and then freeze the top 100 rows, you can't see rows 1 to 99 anymore.

Tip: Freezing splits a worksheet into multiple **panes**—separate frames that each provide a different view of the same worksheet.

To freeze rows or columns:

- Do any of the following:

    ▸ To freeze the first row, tap View tab > Freeze Panes > Freeze Top Row.

    ▸ To freeze the leftmost column, tap View tab > Freeze Panes > Freeze First Column.

    ▸ To freeze columns and rows at the same time, select the cell below and to the right of the rows and columns that you want to keep visible, and then tap View tab > Freeze Panes > Freeze Panes (Figure 3.32).

    ▸ To unfreeze panes, tap View tab > Freeze Panes and then clear all the selected options.

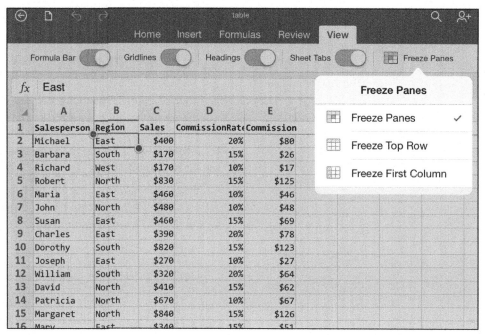

Figure 3.32 Freezing rows and columns.

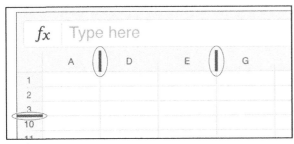

Figure 3.33 Thick bars indicate hidden row or columns.

Hiding rows and columns

Hiding rows and columns doesn't delete data; it just keeps it out of sight. For example, you can hide a column of numbers that you need only for a calculation but don't want to see when you edit or print the worksheet. Think of hidden rows or columns as having a row height or column width of zero.

To hide rows or columns:

1 Select the row(s) or column(s) that you want to hide. If you select a range of rows or columns, they'll all be hidden.

2 Tap Hide on the pop-up menu.

   Thick bars in the row or column headings indicate that some row numbers or column letters are hidden (Figure 3.33).

To unhide (show) rows or columns:

1 Select the *range* of rows or columns that includes the hidden cells. To unhide columns B and C, for example, select columns A and D.

2 Tap Unhide on the pop-up menu.

   Excel makes the missing columns or rows visible, and then selects them so that you can see which data you restored.

CHAPTER 4

Entering and Formatting Data

This chapter describes how to work with cells and their contents. The first task in building a workbook is to enter your raw data into a worksheet grid. Each cell can hold a numeric or text value. (Formulas, which are mathematical and functional expressions that resolve to values, are covered in Chapter 5.) In addition to the standard alphabetic keyboard, Excel provides a specialized numeric keyboard that lets you edit and navigate cells quickly. Excel for iPad also supports common operations for entering and managing data: copy and move cells, fill series of values, and sort rows.

Editing Cells

A virtual keyboard appears onscreen whenever you tap any editable area. Keyboards reorient for portrait (tall) and landscape (wide) views. Typing is straightforward and works the same way as typing in other apps.

You enter different types of data by using Excel's different keyboards, accessed by tapping the toggle buttons at the top-right corner of the keyboard. Tap Abc to use the **alphabetic keyboard** or tap 123 to use the **numeric keyboard**. The alphabetic keyboard (Figure 4.1) is the standard iPad keyboard for typing letters, numbers, punctuation, and symbols. The numeric keyboard (Figure 4.2) is a specialized, Excel-only keyboard for typing numbers and symbols, entering formulas and mathematical expressions, and navigating cells.

To edit the contents of a cell:

1. Double-tap the cell. Cell contents appears in the formula bar above the worksheet grid (Figure 4.2).

   or

   If the cell is already selected, tap the formula bar.

2. Use the keyboard to edit the cell's contents, or tap in the formula bar to open a pop-up menu of editing commands.

   You can tap Abc or 123 to switch keyboards at any time.

3. When you're done, move to or tap a different cell, or tap ✓ to dismiss the keyboard. To cancel and revert to the cell's previous contents, tap ✗.

To move from cell to cell when editing cell contents:

1. Tap 123 to show the numeric keyboard.

2. Tap the Return key ↵ (to move down one row), the Tab key (to move right one column), or the arrow keys (to move in any direction).

Tip: If you're in the last column of a table (Chapter 6), tapping the Tab key moves to first cell in the next row, adding a row to the table if necessary.

To clear the contents of cells:

- Select a cell or a range of cells and then tap Clear on the pop-up menu (Figure 4.3).

   Clearing cells removes only their contents; formatting and styles aren't removed.

Figure 4.1 The standard alphabetic keyboard.

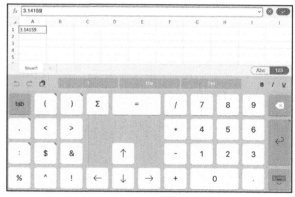

Figure 4.2 Double-tap a cell to edit its contents in the formula bar.

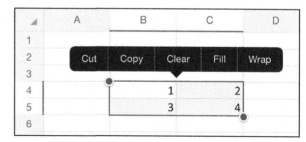

Figure 4.3 Tap Clear to erase cell contents.

Figure 4.4 Press and hold a key to type alternate characters.

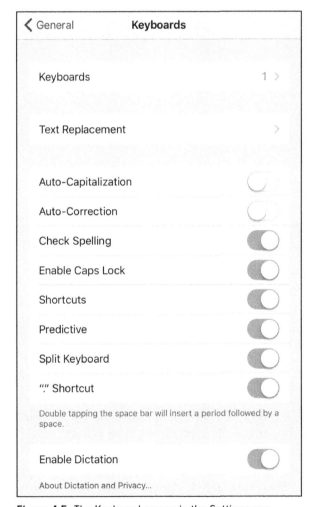

Figure 4.5 The Keyboard screen in the Settings app.

Typing text

The alphabetic keyboard ⌨Abc lets you type text in cells, text boxes, and shapes. Three types of alphabetic keyboards are available: letters, numbers-and-punctuation, and symbols keyboards.

- You can touch and hold certain keys to see variants of their characters in a pop-up display. The E key, for example, lets you type not only the standard e but also ë, é, è, ê, and other diacritics (Figure 4.4).

Tip: The numeric keyboard shares this feature: touch and hold any key that has a green notch in its corner to type alternate characters.

- In the letters keyboard, tap the .?123 key to see numbers and most punctuation; within that layout, tap the #+= key to see less-common symbols, tap 123 to return to the numbers-and-punctuation layout, or tap ABC to return to the letter keys.

- A quick way to type a character on the numbers-and-punctuation or symbols keyboard is to touch and hold the .?123 or #+= key and (still touching the screen) slide your finger up to the character that you want, and then lift your finger. (Characters are typed only when you lift your finger.)

- To delete the last character that you typed, tap ⌫.

- To dismiss the keyboard, tap the ⌨ key.

- To dictate text, tap the 🎤 key.

- To adjust keyboard behavior, on your Home screen, tap Settings > General > Keyboard (Figure 4.5).

Chapter 4 Entering and Formatting Data 53

Selecting and editing text

The basic text-editing operations are:

- **Select** highlights text to edit, cut, copy, or format.
- **Cut and paste** removes (cuts) content and places it in the clipboard so that it can be moved (pasted) elsewhere. Cutting deletes the content and formatting from its original location.
- **Copy and paste** copies content to the clipboard so that it can be duplicated (pasted) elsewhere. Copying leaves the original content and formatting intact (nothing visible happens).

Tip: The select, cut, copy, and paste operations also apply to cells, rows, columns, charts, pictures, text boxes, shapes, and add-ins.

You can select any portion of text within a cell, text box, shape, or text field and then edit it by typing or by using the standard cut, copy, and paste operations in the formula bar:

- When you tap text in an editable area, a blinking **insertion point** indicates where new text will appear when you type or paste.
- Excel's templates (page 31) contain **text placeholders**. Double-tap a placeholder to replace its text with your own.
- To move the insertion point, touch and hold near where you want to place it until a magnifying glass appears, and then drag over the text to the new position and lift your finger (Figure 4.6).
- To select a word, double-tap it.

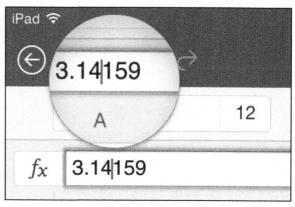

Figure 4.6 Touch and hold text to magnify it.

The Clipboard

The clipboard is the invisible area of memory where Excel stores cut or copied content, where it remains until it's overwritten when you cut or copy something else. This scheme lets you paste the same content multiple times in different places. You can transfer content from Excel to another program—such as Word or PowerPoint—provided that program can read content generated by Excel. Note that you can't paste something that you've deleted or cleared (as opposed to cut), because Excel doesn't place deleted or cleared content in the clipboard.

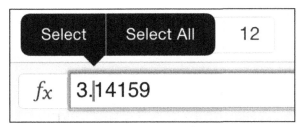

Figure 4.7 The pop-up menu for the insertion point.

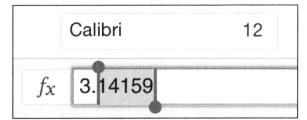

Figure 4.8 Drag the blue handles to change the selection.

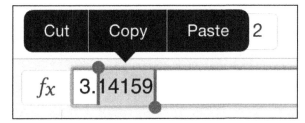

Figure 4.9 The pop-up menu for selected text.

- To open the selection pop-up menu, tap once in an editable area, and then tap again in the same place (Figure 4.7). The Select command selects the current word. The Select All command selects all the text.

- To extend or shorten the range of selected text, select a word and then drag or flick the blue selection handles ● to encompass the characters or paragraphs that you want to select (Figure 4.8). When you drag beyond the edge of the current paragraph, the selection changes to contain the entire paragraph; you can drag the selection handles up or down to select multiple paragraphs (flick to exit paragraph selection).

- To cut or copy text, select a range of text, tap Cut or Copy, move the insertion point (or select some text to replace), and then tap Paste (Figure 4.9).

- Buttons on the **shortcut bar** (above the keyboard) provide quick, context-sensitive access to common commands such as bold, italic, copy, paste, and undo. To toggle shortcuts, on the Home screen, tap Settings > General > Keyboard > Shortcuts.

- If you make a mistake, use the Undo command in the ribbon.

Selecting Text Quickly

On iOS 9 or later, you can use the onscreen keyboard as a trackpad to select text quickly.

- To move the insertion point, touch the keyboard with two fingers, maintaining contact with the glass. The keyboard darkens and all the keys turn blank. Drag both fingers anywhere on the screen and then lift them when the insertion point is where you want it.

- To select text, move the insertion point to where you want the selection to begin (or end), and then double-tap the keyboard with two fingers, maintaining contact with the glass. The nearest word is selected. Drag both fingers to extend the selection.

In some editing contexts, you can touch or double-tap two fingers anywhere on the screen, not only on the keyboard.

Tip: These features are easier to use if you spread both fingers slightly before touching the screen.

Using an External Keyboard

Using an external keyboard (such as the Apple Wireless Keyboard) with your iPad lets you use many of the same keyboard shortcuts that you're familiar with if you also use Office for Windows or Mac. The Office for Windows keyboard shortcut to copy text, for example, is Ctrl+C, but on the iPad, you'd press Command+C. Table 4.1 lists the keyboard shortcuts that work in Excel for iPad.

Tip: To set up a wireless keyboard, on your Home screen, tap Settings > Bluetooth, and then pair your keyboard and iPad.

Table 4.1 Keyboard Shortcuts for Excel for iPad

To	Press
Move one cell to the right	Tab key
Move one cell up, down, left, or right	Arrow keys
Move within cell text	Arrow keys
Cut, Copy, Paste	Command+X, Command+C, Command+V
Undo	Command+Z
Redo	Command+Y or Command+Shift+Z
Bold, Italic, Underline	Command+B, Command+I, Command+U
Select all	Command+A
Select a range of cells	Shift+arrow key
Insert a line break within a cell	Alt+Return
Move cursor to the beginning of the current line within a cell	Command+left arrow
Move cursor to the end of the current line within a cell	Command+right arrow
Move cursor to the beginning of the current cell	Command+up arrow
Move cursor to the end of the current cell	Command+down arrow
Within a cell that contains a line break, move cursor up by one paragraph	Option+up arrow
Within a cell that contains a line break, move cursor down by one paragraph	Option+down arrow
Move cursor right by one word	Option + right arrow
Move cursor left by one word	Option + left arrow

Using Editing Tools

You can find every instance of a word or phrase in your worksheet or workbook and optionally change it to something else.

To find or replace text:

1. Tap Q in the ribbon (Figure 4.10).

2. In the search field, type the text that you want to find. The number of matches appears on the right side of the search field. You can tap in the field to show a pop-up menu of the standard editing commands (cut, copy, paste, and so on).

3. To constrain the search area, tap ⚙ and then tap Workbook (to search every worksheet) or Sheet (to search only the current worksheet).

4. To constrain the search results, tap ⚙ and then turn on Match Case (for case-sensitive matches) or Match Cell (to match the entire cell contents).

5. To replace the found text with new text, tap ⚙, tap Find and Replace, and then type the new text in the Replace field.

6. Do any of the following:

   ▸ To find the next or previous instance of the text, tap ⟩ or ⟨.

   ▸ To replace the current instance of the text, tap Replace.

   ▸ To replace all instances of the text, tap All.

   ▸ To exit Find and Replace, tap a cell.

Figure 4.10 Use Find and Replace to search for instances of matching text in a worksheet or workbook.

Chapter 4 Entering and Formatting Data 57

Working with Comments

Comments are notes that make a worksheet easier to understand by providing additional context for the data it contains. Comments are often used to call out unusual or summary values, make personal notes, query reviewers or collaborators, and insert editorial or proofreading suggestions.

You can add, edit, view, or delete comments. To add a comment to a cell, select the cell and then tap Review tab > Comment (or Insert tab > Comment). When a cell has a comment, a tiny red indicator appears in the corner of the cell. To show or hide the Comments pane, tap Review tab > Show Comments. Alternatively, select any cell that has a comment and then tap the pop-up comment icon. Use the Comments pane to select, edit, or delete comments (Figure 4.11).

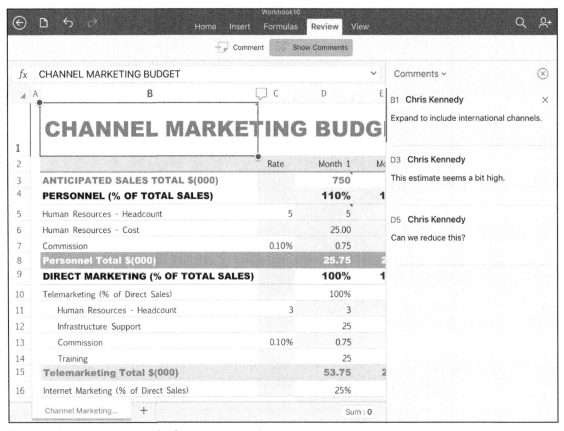

Figure 4.11 A worksheet with the Comments pane showing.

Formatting and Styling Cells

You can apply a format to a cell to display its value in a particular way. Applying a currency format, for example, displays a currency symbol (such as $, £, €, or ¥) next to numbers in cells. To make a cell stand out, you can change its style (typeface, color, alignment, border, and so on). Cell formats and styles determine only how cell values are *displayed*; the actual values aren't changed.

You can format empty cells. When you enter a value in the cell, it's displayed using the cell's format. Clearing a cell (tapping Clear on the pop-up menu) removes its contents but not its formatting; deleting a cell (tapping a Delete command on the Home tab's Insert & Delete Cells menu) removes both.

Formats and styles are applied by using the Home tab in the ribbon (Figure 4.12).

You can also copy and paste only formatting (without values or formulas), which is faster than repeatedly slogging through formatting commands on the Home tab.

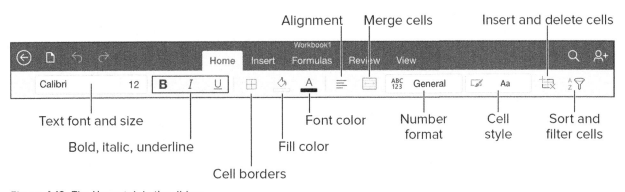

Figure 4.12 The Home tab in the ribbon.

To format cells:

1. Select a cell or a range of cells to format.
2. Tap the Home tab in the ribbon.
3. Tap the Number Formatting button. The button's icon and label indicate the current format of the active cell. The default format is General (Figure 4.13).
4. To apply a default format quickly, tap a format name in the menu.

   or

   To set options for a format, tap ⓘ next to the format name in the menu. Depending on the format, you can set the number of decimal places, toggle thousands separators, change the appearance of negative values, set the type and placement of currency symbols, display dates and times, show fractions and percentages, format postal codes and telephone numbers, and more.

   Cells update instantly to reflect the formatting options that you choose.

   In Figure 4.14, the three columns show the same value of a number, a date, and a time, respectively, but formatted differently. When a cell is used in a formula, its actual value is used, not its formatted value.

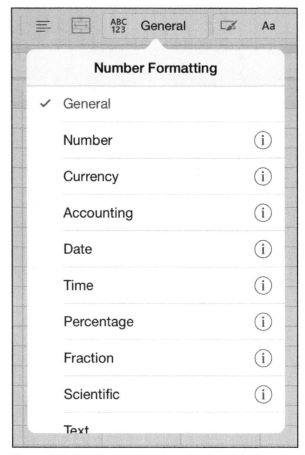

Figure 4.13 The Number Formatting menu on the Home tab.

	1.5	11/5/15	1:30:45 PM
	1.5000	Thursday, November 5, 2015	13:30
	$1.50	11/5	1:30 PM
£	1.50	11/05/15	13:30:45
	€ 1.50	5-Nov	1:30 अ
	1.50 €	5-Nov-15	13時30分
USD	1.50	05-Nov-15	0.563020833
	150.0%	November 5, 2015	
	1 1/2	11/5/15 12:00 AM	
	1 8/16	5-Nov-2015	
	1.50E+00	42313	

Figure 4.14 Examples of formatted cells.

Figure 4.15 The Cell Styles menu.

A	B	C
11	22	33
111	222	333

Figure 4.16 Examples of styled cells.

To style cells:

1. Select a cell or a range of cells to style.
2. Tap the Home tab in the ribbon.
3. To apply a predefined style, tap (Figure 4.15).
4. To apply a custom style, do any of the following on the Home tab:
   - Tap the font buttons to set the font or font size.
   - Tap a typeface button to apply bold, italic, or underline.
   - Tap to put a border around the cells.
   - Tap to choose a background color for the cells.
   - Tap A to choose a text color.
   - Tap to align text horizontally (left, center, or right) or vertically (top, middle, or bottom) within the cell.

   Cells update instantly to reflect the style options that you choose (Figure 4.16).

To copy and paste formats:

1. Select the cell or a range of cells whose format you want to copy.
2. Tap Copy on the pop-up menu.
3. Select another range of cells.
4. Tap Paste Format on the pop-up menu.

   Excel pastes only the formatting, leaving all values and formulas in the paste area unchanged.

Numbers Formatted as Text

By typing an apostrophe (') at the beginning of a number, you can force Excel to format and store it as text instead of as a number. This option comes in handy for text labels that contain only digits (especially codes or identifiers that have leading zeroes).

Numbers can also end up in text format inadvertently. A number that you enter is formatted and stored as text, instead of as a number, when you enter it in a cell that's already formatted as text.

If a cell is formatted with the default General number format, then text you enter in that cell is left-aligned and numbers you enter are right-aligned. Alignment can help you spot numbers that are stored as text, as they will be left-aligned instead of right-aligned. Changing the alignment or other cell formatting options, however, doesn't change how Excel stores a value that's already been entered in a cell. Even changing the number format of a cell won't change a value that's been stored as text into a value stored as a number, or vice versa. To store the value as a number again, you must first reformat the cell with a number format, and then re-enter the number in that reformatted cell.

When you import or paste data into Excel from an external source, such as a database or a webpage, Excel may recognize the type of data as either numbers or text. If the external data source stores numbers as text, Excel may also store them as text. If a field in the external database contains numbers for some records and text for other records, for example, Excel may store the values the same way, so that some of the values in a column of numbers are stored as text.

Though alignment can help you spot numbers that are formatted and stored as text, those values can be large enough to fill the entire cell, making it hard to see whether they're left- or right-aligned. The easiest way to find incorrectly formatted numbers is to sort them and then identify any rows that are out of order.

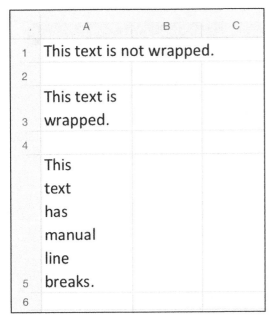

Figure 4.17 Examples of unwrapped and wrapped text.

Figure 4.18 Press and hold the Return key to view the Line Break key.

Wrapping Text in a Cell

If you want text to appear on multiple lines in a cell, you can format the cell so that text wraps automatically, or you can enter a manual line break (Figure 4.17).

To wrap text automatically:

- Select a cell or a range of cells and then tap Wrap on the pop-up menu.

  If the text is already wrapped, tap Unwrap to unwrap it.

Tip: Text wraps to fit the column width. When you change the column width (page 47), text wrapping adjusts automatically.

To enter a manual line break in a cell:

1. Double-tap the cell to edit it.
2. Position the insertion point where you want the text to break.
3. Tap 123 to show the numeric keyboard.
4. Press and hold the Return key ↵ to view additional keys, and then drag your finger to the Line Break key ↓ (Figure 4.18).

Tip: If some wrapped text isn't visible, it may be because the row is set to a specific height (page 47). To let the row adjust automatically to show all wrapped text, select the row and then tap AutoFit on the pop-up menu.

Chapter 4 Entering and Formatting Data 63

Cutting, Copying, and Pasting Cells

You can cut or copy cells and paste them within the same worksheet or to another worksheet. You can also paste cells to a different workbook file—the contents of the clipboard don't change when you close one workbook and open another. For an overview of cut, copy, and paste, see "Selecting and editing text" on page 54.

To cut, copy, and paste cells:

1. Select the range of cells that you want to cut or copy.

2. Tap Cut or Copy on the pop-up menu (Figure 4.19).

3. Select the destination cell(s) and then tap Paste on the pop-up menu.

4. (Optional) Choose a paste option. By default, Excel replaces the values and formatting of the destination cells. For other paste options, tap ▢ near the pasted cells (this icon appears right after you paste) and then choose one of the following commands (which vary by context):

    ▸ **Keep Source Formatting.** Preserve all original formatting of the pasted selection, and preserve all formulas as well. Turning off this setting turns on Match Destination Formatting.

    ▸ **Match Destination Formatting.** Format the pasted cells to match the formatting already existing in the new location.

    ▸ **Paste Values.** If the pasted cells contain formulas, then strip all formulas and paste only their computed values.

    ▸ **Paste Formulas.** Preserve all formulas. See also "Copying and Moving Formulas" on page 94.

    ▸ **Paste as Picture.** Paste the cells as a picture (image).

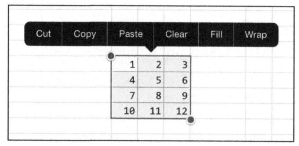

Figure 4.19 The pop-up menu has Cut, Copy, and Paste commands.

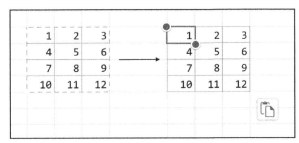

Figure 4.20 Pasting to a one-cell destination.

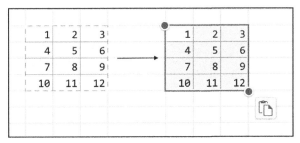

Figure 4.21 Pasting to a same-sized destination.

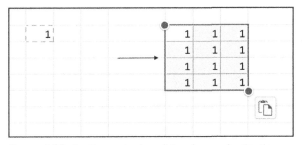

Figure 4.22 Pasting a single cell to a larger destination.

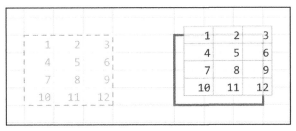

Figure 4.23 Touch and hold selected cells and then drag them to a new destination.

The paste destination determines how Excel pastes the clipboard contents:

- When you select only one destination cell, Excel pastes the entire clipboard, using that cell as the top-left corner of the pasted cells (Figure 4.20).

- When the selected destination has the *same* dimensions (that is, the same number of rows and columns) as the clipboard's contents, Excel pastes the entire clipboard unchanged (Figure 4.21).

- When the selected destination has *smaller* or *larger* dimensions than the clipboard's contents, Excel pastes the entire clipboard unchanged.

- Pasting a single cell to a range of cells clones the original cell in every cell of the destination (Figure 4.22).

To move cells by dragging:

1. Select the range of cells that you want to move.

   You can select a single cell, a block of cells, or entire rows or columns.

2. Touch and hold the selection until it rises out of the worksheet.

   If you selected entire rows or columns, touch and hold a selected cell, not the row or column headings.

3. Drag it to another location in the same worksheet (Figure 4.23).

   A transparent image of the original cells follows your drag. Excel indicates where the selection will land when you lift your finger. (You can't drag to another worksheet.)

Merging Cells

Merging cells combines adjacent cells into one, removing the borders so that they behave as a single cell. Merging is typically used to create a centered column or row heading.

When you merge two or more adjacent horizontal or vertical cells, the cells become one larger cell that's displayed across multiple columns or rows. The contents of only the top-left cell appears in the merged cell. The contents of the other merged cells are deleted.

Formula references in other cells are adjusted automatically to use the cell reference of the merged cell. To refer to a merged cell in a formula, use the address of the merged cell's top-left corner.

After merging cells, you can unmerge (split) a merged cell into separate cells again.

Figure 4.24 shows a block of cells before they're merged (top), after they're merged (middle), and after they're unmerged (bottom). Note that unmerging doesn't restore cell contents that was deleted during the merge.

Tip: Merged cells have little use beyond creating cosmetically appealing headings. You can't sort a range containing merged cells or merge cells in a table (Chapter 6).

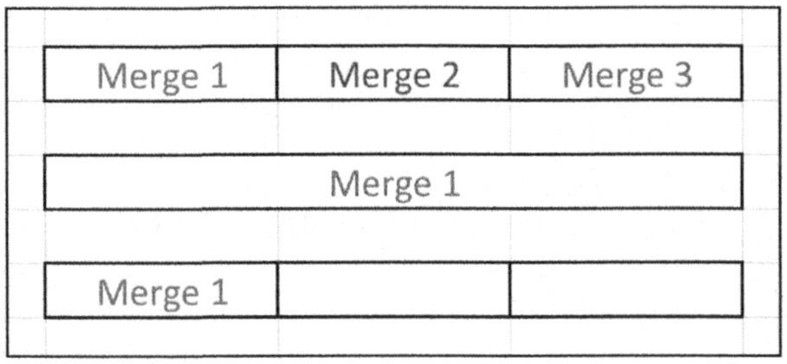

Figure 4.24 Pre-merged, merged, and unmerged cells.

To merge cells:

1 Select a range of two or more adjacent cells to merge.

2 Tap the Home tab in the ribbon and then tap the Merge button ⇄.

To unmerge cells:

1 Select a merged cell.

2 Tap the Home tab in the ribbon and then tap the Merge button ⇄.

Filling Cells with Data Series

AutoFill creates a column or row of values based on just one or two (or more) cells that Excel can extrapolate into a series. AutoFill looks at the values that you've already entered in a row or column and infers the additional values to append. AutoFill recognizes standard data series:

- Numbers that regularly increase (1, 2, 3) or decrease (–5, –10, –15)
- Times of day (6:00, 7:00, 8:00)
- Calendar dates (15-Jan, 15-Feb, 15-Mar)
- Days of the week (Sunday, Monday, Tuesday), either written out or in three-letter abbreviations
- Months (Jan, Feb, Mar), either written out or in three-letter abbreviations
- Quarters (Q1, Q2, Q3, Q4), written as Q1 or Qtr1 or Quarter1
- Years (2014, 2015, 2016)
- Ordinal numbers (1st, 2nd, 3rd)
- Alphanumeric serial numbers, where text is followed by digits (Item 1, Item 2, Item 3, or ABC-010, ABC-020, ABC-030)

You can also use AutoFill to copy a single cell multiple times (like a fast copy-and-paste). If you select one cell that contains a number or text that's not part of a standard series, AutoFill will copy that value to all the target cells in the row or column.

If you start with two or more cells containing text that's not part of a standard series, AutoFill simply repeats the pattern. Selecting three adjacent cells containing E, G, and G, for example, fills the target cells with E, G, G, E, G, G,....

If you start with three or more cells containing numbers spaced at irregular intervals, AutoFill extrapolates the pattern linearly (which usually isn't what you want). Selecting three adjacent cells containing 2, 4, and 8, for example, fills the target cells with 2, 4, 8, 10.67, 13.67, 16.67,....

AutoFill doesn't establish an ongoing relationship among cells. After filling, you can change the cells in the filled range independently. When you fill a formula into new cells, Excel updates the formula's cell references to reflect the new locations. For details, see "Copying and Moving Formulas" on page 94.

Figure 4.25 shows before-and-after results of filling columns with different starting values. Note the series in the fifth column (1.33, 1.66,...)—filling decimal (floating-point) numbers can lead to unexpected results due to rounding.

To fill a range of cells:

1. Enter the starting value(s) of the series in a row or column.
2. Select the cell(s) that you just edited.
3. Tap Fill on the pop-up menu.

   AutoFill arrows appear on the selection border.

   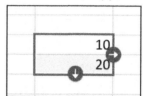

4. Drag a fill arrow down or to the right along the column or row that you want to fill.

   Excel fills the row or column with the next values in the series. If any target cells already contain data, Excel overwrites them with the new values and formats.

   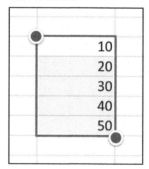

1	10	2	0.0	1.33	1	Feb	Monday	31-Oct-14	1:00 PM	1st Place	Part 5	cat
	11	-2	1.5	1.66	2		Wednesday	30-Nov-14	3:30 PM		Part 10	dog
					6							mouse

↓

1	10	2	0.0	1.33	1	Feb	Monday	31-Oct-14	1:00 PM	1st Place	Part 5	cat
1	11	-2	1.5	1.66	2	Mar	Wednesday	30-Nov-14	3:30 PM	2nd Place	Part 10	dog
1	12	-6	3.0	1.99	6	Apr	Friday	31-Dec-14	6:00 PM	3rd Place	Part 15	mouse
1	13	-10	4.5	2.32	8	May	Sunday	31-Jan-15	8:30 PM	4th Place	Part 20	cat
1	14	-14	6.0	2.65	10.5	Jun	Tuesday	28-Feb-15	11:00 PM	5th Place	Part 25	dog
1	15	-18	7.5	2.98	13	Jul	Thursday	31-Mar-15	1:30 AM	6th Place	Part 30	mouse
1	16	-22	9.0	3.31	15.5	Aug	Saturday	30-Apr-15	4:00 AM	7th Place	Part 35	cat
1	17	-26	10.5	3.64	18	Sep	Monday	31-May-15	6:30 AM	8th Place	Part 40	dog
1	18	-30	12.0	3.97	20.5	Oct	Wednesday	30-Jun-15	9:00 AM	9th Place	Part 45	mouse
1	19	-34	13.5	4.30	23	Nov	Friday	31-Jul-15	11:30 AM	10th Place	Part 50	cat

Figure 4.25 Examples of filled cells.

Sorting Data

Sorting data in cells makes values easier to find and patterns easier to spot.

- You can sort in ascending order (A, B, C…1, 2, 3…Jan, Feb, Mar) or descending order (Z, Y, X…3, 2, 1…Dec, Nov, Oct).

- You can sort any values: numbers, text, dates, and so on. For text values, sorting is case-sensitive.

- If you sort data that includes text and numbers, Excel sorts the text values separately from the number values. Logical (TRUE/FALSE) values are also sorted separately. If numbers are formatted as text (page 62), then they are sorted as text values instead of as numbers (which can cause unexpected results).

- Empty cells always sort last, no matter how they're formatted.

- If you select a column of data to sort that's adjacent to other (non-empty) columns of data—as in a table (Chapter 6)—then the whole rectangular region is sorted. Entire rows stay intact when they jump to their new sorted positions in the tabular range. Excel doesn't sort the header row, if present.

To sort data:

1 Select the range of cells that you want to sort (Figure 4.26).

2 Tap the Home tab in the ribbon, tap the Sort and Filter button $^A_Z \triangledown$, and then tap Ascending or Descending (Figure 4.27).

Multicolumn sorts

Unlike Excel for Windows or Mac, Excel for iPad doesn't support multicolumn sorts, which are used to break ties when two or more rows have the same value in a sort column. But there's a workaround: to do a multicolumn sort on the columns A, B, and C, for example, work backward: first sort on column C, then B, and then A. This technique works because Excel retains the order of rows when sorting tied values.

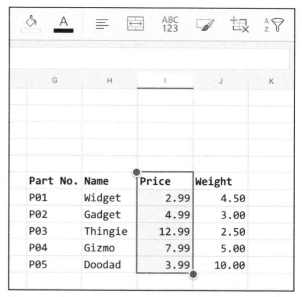

Figure 4.26 A rectangular range sorted by part number.

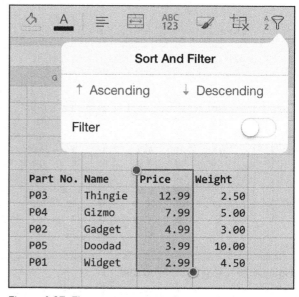

Figure 4.27 The same range sort by price.

70 Excel for iPad & iPad Pro

CHAPTER 5

Formulas and Functions

After you enter and organize your data values in tables, you can use formulas and functions to transform raw numbers to meaningful information. A **formula** performs a calculation and displays the result in the cell where you enter the formula, called a **formula cell**. Formulas can do things as simple as adding two numbers, but functions are the real power of spreadsheets. **Functions** are built-in, named operations, such as SUM and TRIM, that perform a wide range of calculations for math, statistics, dates and times, text, finance, engineering, logic, and more.

Formula Basics

A formula cell displays the result of its calculation and, on the surface, looks like any other (nonformula) cell. By just looking at a worksheet, you can't tell the difference between a cell that contains a formula whose result is 3 and a cell that contains the number 3 (the number typed in directly). It's crucial to distinguish a formula's two display components: the formula itself and the resulting value. The actual contents of a formula cell is an equation—the formula—that tells Excel how to generate that cell's value. It's that value, and not the formula, that's used in any calculations that refer to the cell.

- You enter each formula into a single cell. A formula can **reference** other cells in the workbook, but the entire formula itself resides only in the cell where its result is displayed.

- Excel recalculates the result of a formula every time you open a workbook or change a data value that the formula uses. In Figure 5.1, for example, if you change any Test 1 score, Excel auto-updates the values of the formula cells showing that column's average, maximum, and minimum , as well as the values in the column F formulas that calculate overall averages. For small worksheets or simple formulas, updates occur instantly; for large worksheets or complex formulas, updates are slower.

- Formulas can operate on and display results in any data type: numbers, text, dates, and so on.

> **Recalculating Manually**
>
> To force all worksheets in the open workbook to recalculate, tap the Calculate Now button on the Formulas tab in the ribbon. This button, which is the equivalent of the F9 key in Excel for Windows or Mac, is useful for forcing volatile functions to update. A **volatile function** is one whose returned value can't be assumed to be the same from one moment to the next even if none of its arguments (if it takes any) has changed. Excel reevaluates cells that contain volatile functions, together with all dependents, every time that it recalculates. Volatile functions slow recalculation times and should be used sparingly. Excel's volatile functions are NOW, TODAY, RAND, RANDBETWEEN, OFFSET, INDIRECT, INFO (depending on its arguments), and CELL (depending on its arguments).

To view a formula:

- Tap the cell containing the formula.

    Excel displays the cell's formula in the **formula bar** above the worksheet grid. The formula bar lets you view, as well as edit, formulas. Figure 5.1 shows students' test scores. The selected cell in the second column (cell address B8) shows the average scores of all five students on the first test. The formula bar shows the actual contents of the cell (which uses the AVERAGE function), and the cell itself displays the formula's result (81).

Tip: To show or hide the formula bar, tap View tab > Formula Bar.

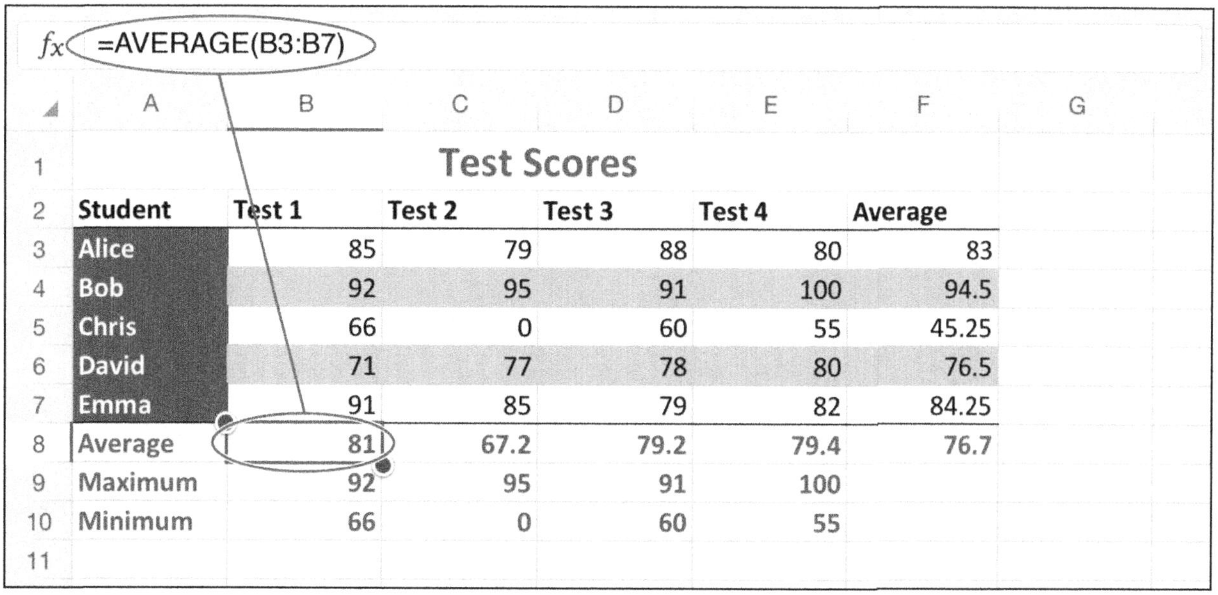

f_x =AVERAGE(B3:B7)

	A	B	C	D	E	F	G
1			Test Scores				
2	Student	Test 1	Test 2	Test 3	Test 4	Average	
3	Alice	85	79	88	80	83	
4	Bob	92	95	91	100	94.5	
5	Chris	66	0	60	55	45.25	
6	David	71	77	78	80	76.5	
7	Emma	91	85	79	82	84.25	
8	Average	81	67.2	79.2	79.4	76.7	
9	Maximum	92	95	91	100		
10	Minimum	66	0	60	55		
11							

Figure 5.1 The formula bar lets you view and edit formulas.

Parts of a Formula

Every formula uses some combination of the elements shown in Figure 5.2.

Equal sign (=). An equal sign is required at the start of every formula.

Constants. Constants, also called literals or static values, are numbers or text values. Constants never change unless you edit them explicitly in a formula. Surround text constants in formulas with double quotes.

Arithmetic operators. These operators do basic math. The **unary arithmetic operators** work on only one numeric value (Table 5.1). The **binary arithmetic operators** work on two numeric values (Table 5.2).

Cell references. These references point to the cell or range of cells whose values you need to do a calculation. See "Cell References" on page 79.

Comparison operators. These operators compare two values and return a logical (true/false) value depending on their relationship (equal, not equal, less than, and so on). See "Comparison Operators" on page 85.

Functions. Functions built into Excel let you do a wide range of calculations. The TODAY function, for example, returns today's date, and STDEV calculates the sample standard deviation of a range of numbers. See "Functions" on page 88.

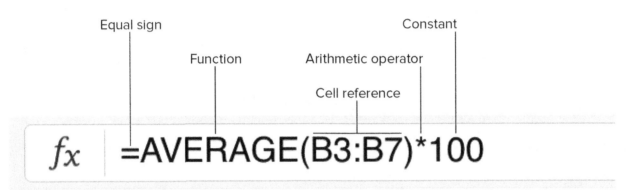

Figure 5.2 The parts of a formula.

Table 5.1 Unary Arithmetic Operators

Operator	Description	Example	Result
−	The **negation operator** reverses the sign (positive or negative) of a value	8 + −2	6
+	The **identity operator** leaves a value unchanged (rarely useful)	8 − +2	6
%	The **percent operator** divides a value by 100	2%	0.02 (formatted as 2%)

Table 5.2 Binary Arithmetic Operators

Operator	Description	Example	Result
+	The **addition operator** adds two values	2 + 4	6
−	The **subtraction operator** subtracts the second value from the first	2 − 4	−2
*	The **multiplication operator** multiplies two values	2 * 4	8
/	The **division operator** divides first value by the second	2 / 4	0.5
^	The **exponentiation operator** raises the first value to the power of the second	2 ^ 4	16

Entering Formulas

The simplest type of formula sets a cell value equal to a constant, but typing =2 is no different than just typing 2 in a cell—no formula needed. Nontrivial formulas use operators and functions. The formula =1+1 uses the addition operator to sum two constants. The leading equal sign distinguishes a formula from numbers and text values. When entering a formula, you can use most of the standard editing techniques described in "Editing Cells" on page 52.

The formula bar (above the worksheet grid) always displays the complete formula. You can type formulas on any of Excel's different keyboards, accessed by tapping the toggle buttons at the top-right corner of the keyboard. Tap `Abc` to use the alphabetic keyboard or tap `123` to use the numeric keyboard. The alphabetic keyboard is the standard iPad keyboard for typing letters, numbers, punctuation, and symbols. The numeric keyboard is a specialized, Excel-only keyboard for typing numbers and symbols, entering formulas and mathematical expressions, and navigating cells.

To enter a formula in a cell:

1. Double-tap the cell.

    or

    If the cell is already selected, tap the formula bar.

    The keyboard opens automatically. You can tap `Abc` or `123` to switch keyboards at any time.

2. If you're entering a new formula, type = to start the formula.

    or

    If you're editing an existing formula, Excel selects the whole formula in the formula bar.

3. Position the insertion point in the formula bar or select an element to change or replace, and then do any of the following (Figure 5.3):

    ▸ To insert a constant value, type it. Surround text constants in formulas with double quotes.

    ▸ To insert an arithmetic operator (page 74), type it. (The numeric keyboard provides the quickest access to operators.)

    ▸ To insert a cell reference, see "Cell References" on page 79.

    ▸ To insert a comparison operator, see "Comparison Operators" on page 85.

    ▸ To insert a function, see "Functions" on page 88.

    ▸ To remove an element, select it or position the insertion point to the right of the element, and then tap ⌫. To remove multiple elements, tap repeatedly or touch and hold ⌫.

4. When you're done, tap ✓ to enter the formula, or tap ✕ to cancel and revert to the cell's previous contents.

Tip: The formula bar expands automatically to make it easier to view or edit a long formula or large amount of text in a cell. To shrink the formula bar back to its normal size, tap ⌃ on the right side of the formula bar.

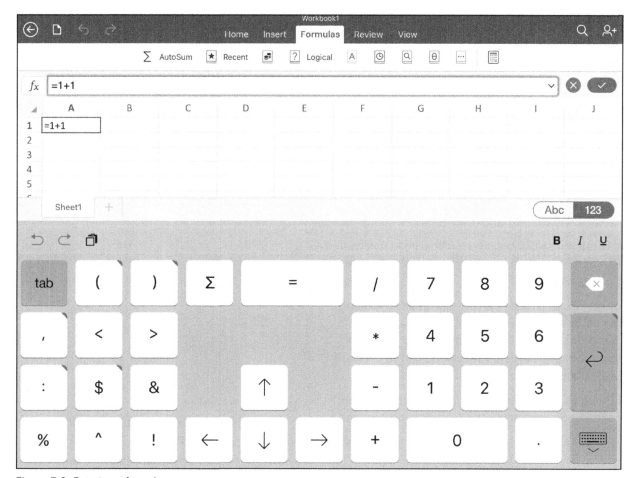

Figure 5.3 Entering a formula.

Saving Formulas

Instead of tapping ✓ to save your formula and dismiss the keyboard, you can move from cell to cell and enter more formulas. On the numeric keyboard, tap the Return key ↵ (to move down one row), the Tab key (to move right one column), or the arrow keys (to move in any direction).

You can also tap another cell to save the formula and select the tapped cell. If the formula is incomplete or if an argument or placeholder is selected, however, tapping another cell inserts a reference to that cell in the formula itself. For example, if you type the incomplete formula =1+ in cell A1 and then tap cell A2, then Excel changes the formula to =1+A2 and stays in editing mode in cell A1. If you type the complete formula =1+1 in cell A1 and then tap cell A2, then Excel saves the formula in cell A1 and selects cell A2.

Evaluation Order

Excel uses rules of precedence and associativity to determine the order in which it evaluates each part of an arithmetic formula.

Precedence

Precedence determines the priority of various operators when more than one operator is used in a formula. Operations with higher precedence are performed first. The formula

=2+3*4

is 14 rather than 20 because multiplication has higher precedence than addition. Excel first calculates 3 * 4 and then adds 2.

Operators with lower precedence are less **binding** than those with higher precedence. Table 5.3 lists operator precedences from most to least binding; operators in the same row of the list have equal precedence.

Arithmetic operators have higher precedence than comparison operators but lower precedence than functions.

Associativity

Associativity determines the order of evaluation in a formula when adjacent operators have equal precedence. Excel uses left-to-right associativity for all operators, so

=6/2*3

is 9 (not 1) because 6/2 is evaluated first, and

=2^3^2

is 64 (not 512) because 2^3 is evaluated first.

Table 5.3 Order of Evaluation (Highest to Lowest)

Operator	Description
()	Calculations inside parentheses
–, +	Unary negation, unary identity
%	Percent
^	Exponentiation
*, /	Multiplication, division
+, –	Addition, subtraction

Using Parentheses to Control Evaluation Order

You can use parentheses to override precedence and associativity rules. Expressions inside parentheses are evaluated before expressions outside them. Adding parentheses to the preceding examples, you get (2+3)*4 is 20, 6/(2*3) is 1, and 2^(3^2) is 512. It's good practice to add parentheses (even when they're unnecessary) to lengthy formulas to ensure your intended evaluation order and make formulas easier to read.

=5^2*4/2

is equivalent to

=((5^2)*4)/2

but the latter formula is clearer.

Use parentheses in pairs (one closing parenthesis for every opening one). If you mismatch parentheses, Excel will correct the formula automatically or, failing that, flag a formula error.

Cell References

The real power of formulas comes from using cell references to identify (point to) cells whose values you want to use.

Cell reference basics

At the top and left edges of a worksheet grid are **headings** that identify columns and rows. **Column headings** use letters to refer to columns, and **row headings** use numbers to refer to rows. In Figure 5.4, cell B2 is selected.

Tip: To show or hide column and row headings, tap View tab > Headings.

Each **cell reference** is an address named for the column–row intersection where the cell is located. B2, for example, is the cell at the intersection of column B and row 2. A range of cells is identified by a pair of cell references separated by a colon (:). A1:B3, for example, refers to the rectangular block of six cells between A1 and B3 inclusive—that is, cells A1, A2, A3, B1, B2, and B3.

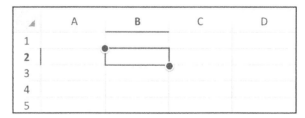

Figure 5.4 Column and row headings change color to show which cells are selected.

The first 26 columns of the worksheet grid are labeled from A to Z. Column 27 is labeled AA, column 28 is AB, and so on. Cell BC500, for example, is located at the intersection of column 55 and row 500.

A cell reference in a formula tells Excel to get that cell's value and use it in the formula's calculation. The simplest example is

=A1

which sets the value of the formula cell to whatever value is in cell A1. You can treat cell references like ordinary values. The formula

=A1*2

returns twice the value of A1, provided that A1 holds a number.

The formula in Figure 5.5 references multiple cells. The formula cell, C3, sums the values in the four cells A1, B1, A2, and B2, which are temporarily color-coded to match the colors used in the formula bar. Formulas always reflect the current state of the spreadsheet. If you change any value in the range A1:B2, Excel recalculates the result in C3 automatically.

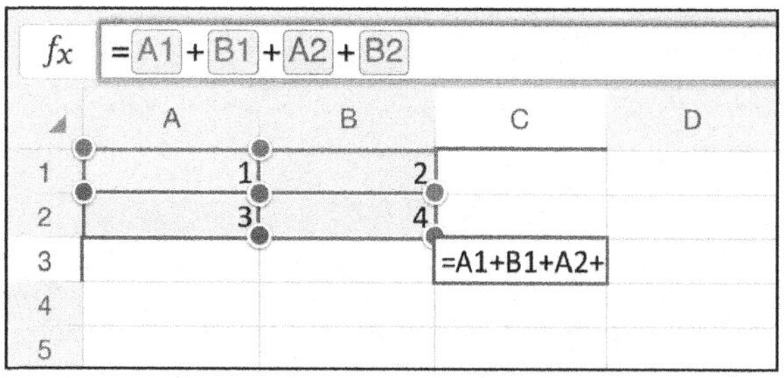

Reference operators

You can use the following **reference operators** to combine ranges of cells for calculations.

- The colon (:) is the **range operator**, which produces one reference to all the cells between two references, including the two references. The colon is by far the most commonly used reference operator. Example: B5:B10.

- The comma (,) is the **union operator**, which combines multiple references into one reference. Unlike elements in mathematical (set theory) unions, cells in Excel unions are counted more than once if they lie in overlapping ranges. Example: SUM(B5:B10,D5:D10).

- A single-space character ( ) is the **intersection operator**, which produces one reference to cells common to the two references. Using this operator incorrectly causes a #NULL! error. Example: B1:B3 A2:C2 (whose intersection is cell B2).

Figure 5.5 A formula referencing multiple cells.

Cell reference formats

Referenced cells can be in the same worksheet as the formula cell, or in another worksheet. Cell references have different formats, depending on whether they refer to a single cell, a range of cells, an entire column or row, another worksheet, and so on. Table 5.4 lists formats for cell references.

Table 5.4 Formats for Cell References

Reference	Format	Example
A cell in the same worksheet that contains the formula	The cell's column letter followed by its row number.	D3 refers to the third row in the fourth column.
A range of cells	*cell_address_1:cell_address_2*	D1:E4 refers to the first four cells in both the fourth and fifth columns (eight cells total).
All cells in a column	*column_letter:column_letter*	C:C refers to all the cells in the third column.
All cells in multiple columns	*column_letter_1:column_letter_2*	B:D refers to all the cells in the second, third, and fourth columns.
All cells in a row	*row_number:row_number*	2:2 refers to all the cells in the second row.
All cells in multiple rows	*row_number_1:row_number_2*	1:5 refers to all the cells in the first five rows. 1:1048576 refers to all cells in a worksheet.
A range in another worksheet	*worksheet_name!cell_reference* If the worksheet name contains spaces, surround the name with single quotes.	Sheet1!C5 and 'Balance Sheet'!A1:C4.
A range in another workbook	*[workbook_file_name]worksheet_name!cell_reference* If the workbook or worksheet name contains spaces, surround both names with one set of single quotes. Excel for iPad doesn't support links to external workbooks.	[Book1.xlsx]Sheet1!C5 and '[Budget 2016.xlsx]Balance Sheet'!A1:C4.

Inserting cell references

When you build a formula, you can type a cell reference manually or let Excel insert it when you select cells. A reference appears in the formula bar as a colored placeholder holding the address or name of the cell(s). The color of each placeholder is coordinated to match the highlight color of the corresponding cells in the worksheet. In Figure 5.6, cell D6 references the two cells to its left. Color-matching makes it clear which cells you're using in the formula. Color highlighting appears only when you're editing a formula.

To redefine a cell reference in a formula, double-tap the cell containing the formula and then drag the color-coded circular **selection handles** in the corners of a block of referenced cells in the worksheet (Figure 5.7). You can drag the handles to expand, shrink, or move the range.

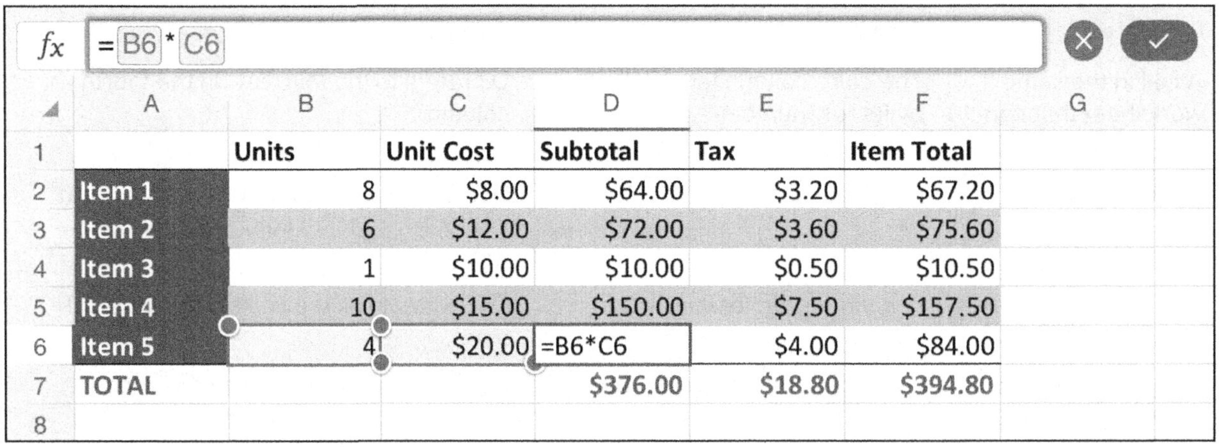

	A	B	C	D	E	F	G
		Units	Unit Cost	Subtotal	Tax	Item Total	
2	Item 1	8	$8.00	$64.00	$3.20	$67.20	
3	Item 2	6	$12.00	$72.00	$3.60	$75.60	
4	Item 3	1	$10.00	$10.00	$0.50	$10.50	
5	Item 4	10	$15.00	$150.00	$7.50	$157.50	
6	Item 5	4	$20.00	=B6*C6	$4.00	$84.00	
7	TOTAL				$376.00	$18.80	$394.80

fx = B6 * C6

Figure 5.6 When you double-tap a cell containing a formula, color-coded cell references are highlighted in the worksheet grid and formula bar.

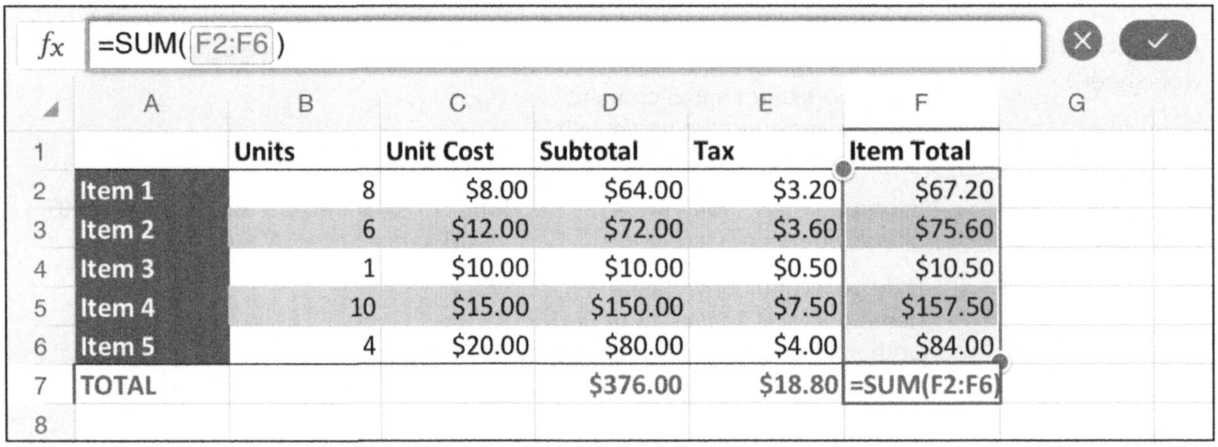

fx =SUM(F2:F6)

	A	B	C	D	E	F	G
1		Units	Unit Cost	Subtotal	Tax	Item Total	
2	Item 1	8	$8.00	$64.00	$3.20	$67.20	
3	Item 2	6	$12.00	$72.00	$3.60	$75.60	
4	Item 3	1	$10.00	$10.00	$0.50	$10.50	
5	Item 4	10	$15.00	$150.00	$7.50	$157.50	
6	Item 5	4	$20.00	$80.00	$4.00	$84.00	
7	TOTAL				$376.00	$18.80	=SUM(F2:F6)

Figure 5.7 You can drag selection handles to redefine a range in a formula.

To insert a cell reference in a formula:

1. In the formula bar, position the insertion point where you want the reference to appear or, to replace an existing reference, tap its placeholder to select it.

2. Do any of the following:

   ▸ Type the reference or name manually.

   ▸ To refer to a single cell, tap the cell.

   ▸ To refer to a range of cells, touch and hold a cell in a corner of the range and then drag across the range.

   In Figure 5.8, the reference in the cell F8 formula was created by dragging from cell B3 to cell E7.

▸ To refer to all cells in a column, tap the column heading (letter). To refer to multiple columns, tap a column heading and then drag its selection handle left or right.

▸ To refer to all cells in a row, tap the row heading (number). To refer to multiple rows, tap a row heading and then drag its selection handle up or down.

▸ To refer to every cell in a worksheet, tap the Select All button ◢ in the top-left corner of the worksheet grid.

▸ To refer to cells in a different worksheet, tap the worksheet tab at the bottom of the screen and then select a reference as described above.

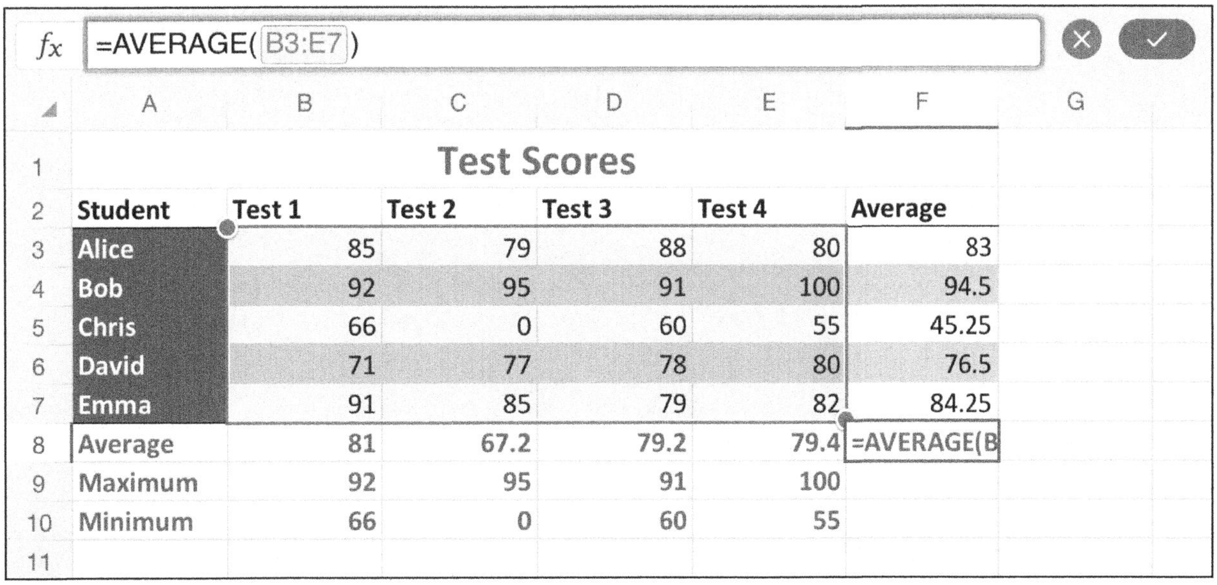

	A	B	C	D	E	F	G
				Test Scores			
2	Student	Test 1	Test 2	Test 3	Test 4	Average	
3	Alice	85	79	88	80	83	
4	Bob	92	95	91	100	94.5	
5	Chris	66	0	60	55	45.25	
6	David	71	77	78	80	76.5	
7	Emma		91	85	79	82	84.25	
8	Average		81	67.2	79.2	79.4	=AVERAGE(B
9	Maximum	92	95	91	100		
10	Minimum	66	0	60	55		
11							

Formula bar: fx =AVERAGE(B3:E7)

Figure 5.8 The highlighted reference spans a range of columns and rows.

Named ranges

Cell and range addresses can be cryptic and confusing when used in formulas. Fortunately, Excel for Windows and Mac let you assign descriptive names to cells and ranges. You can give a cell a name such as interest_rate, for example, or you can name a range MaySales. Named ranges provide several benefits:

- A meaningful range name (such as net_income) is easier to remember than a cell address (such as AB31).

- Names make complex, nested formulas more understandable. A formula such as =(ProductCost + ShippingCost) * MarkupPercentage is more intuitive than =(A30 + B30) * C4.

- Names reduce the likelihood of some types of errors. You're unlikely to notice whether you used B32 instead of B31, for example, but you can spot the wrong name when you use TotalWithTax instead of TaxRate.

- Entering a name is less error prone than entering a cell or range address, and if you mistype a name in a formula, Excel will display a #NAME? error.

- Names use absolute references (page 96). That way, you don't need to worry about having a formula change when you copy a formula from one cell to another. (You *can* break this rule to do some unusual tricks with relative references, but in practice almost all range names use absolute references.)

- Names add an extra layer between your formulas and your worksheet. If you restructure your worksheet, you don't need to modify your formulas. Instead, you simply edit the names so they point to the new cell locations.

Unfortunately, you can't view or edit names in Excel for iPad, but you can use names that are already defined in a workbook. Just type a name where you'd normally enter a cell or range address. If the range A1:A12 is named monthly_sales, for example, you can type =SUM(monthly_sales). If you enter an address that's already named, Excel replaces the address with the name automatically. If you had typed =SUM(A1:A12) in the preceding example, Excel would have changed it to =SUM(monthly_sales) when you saved the formula. To view or edit names in a workbook, use Excel for Windows or Mac.

Comparison Operators

You can use comparison operators to base a formula's result on whether a certain condition is satisfied.

Comparison operator basics

The **comparison operators**, listed in Table 5.5, compare two values and evaluate to TRUE or FALSE (that is, to a logical value). Comparison operators are also called **relational** or **logical operators**.

Comparison operators have lower precedence than arithmetic operators and functions. The expression SUM(A2, B2) + 5 > 10, for example, evaluates as ((SUM(A2, B2)) + 5) > 10. See also "Evaluation Order" on page 78.

Table 5.5 Comparison Operators

Operator	Determines Whether	Example	Result
=	Determines whether two values are equal.	"XYZ" = "xyz"	TRUE
<>	Determines whether two values are not equal.	2 <> 2	FALSE
<	Determines whether the first value is less than the second value.	"ace" < "king"	TRUE
<=	Determines whether the first value is less than or equal to the second value.	1-Dec-2015 <= 1-Nov-2016	TRUE
>	Determines whether the first value is greater than the second value.	2 > 2	FALSE
>=	Determines whether the first value is greater than or equal to the second value.	0 >= −1	TRUE

Logical values

A **logical value**, also called a **boolean value**, indicates one of two states: TRUE or FALSE. In the context of your worksheet, a logical value may mean yes or no, on or off, complete or incomplete, for or against, or alive or dead, but in cells and formulas logical values are either TRUE or FALSE.

You can enter a constant logical value by typing TRUE or FALSE in a cell or formula. For compatibility with other (older) spreadsheet programs, you can instead use the TRUE() and FALSE() functions, which take no arguments and simply return logical TRUE and FALSE, respectively.

In formulas and sorting operations, the value of TRUE is one (1) and FALSE is 0 (zero). To the confusion of many, however, Excel treats logical values in formulas inconsistently. Suppose that cells A1, A2, and A3 contain the logical values TRUE, FALSE, and TRUE, respectively. Then

   =A1+A2+A3 returns 2

but

   =SUM(A1:A3) returns 0

Also,

   =SUM(A1,A2,A3) returns 0

but

   =SUM(TRUE,FALSE,TRUE) returns 2

Note that SUM doesn't coerce logical values in range arguments into ones and zeroes, but does coerce constant TRUE and FALSE arguments into ones and zeroes. A reliable way to count the number of TRUEs in a range is

   =COUNTIF(A1:A3,TRUE)

Tip: A common trick is to multiply a number by a logical value to force the result to be zero if the logical value is FALSE.

Data types in comparisons

The data type determines how values are compared:

- Numeric values compare arithmetically. < means *smaller*, and > means *larger*.

Tip: To compare floating-point numbers for equality, use the DELTA function, or ROUND numbers before comparing them to account for precision errors.

- Text strings compare lexicographically. < means *precedes*, and > means *follows*. Text comparisons are case-insensitive.

Tip: To do a case-sensitive comparison, use the EXACT function.

- Dates and times compare chronologically. < means *earlier*, and > means *later*.

Tip: Excel stores date and time values as numbers internally. For example, 24-Apr-2016 is the integer serial number 42484, 12 noon is decimal number 0.5 (the fraction of a whole day), and 24-Apr-2016 12:00:00 PM is 42484.5. Hence comparing two dates is the same as comparing two numbers internally.

- For logical values, TRUE > FALSE (and FALSE < TRUE) because TRUE is interpreted as 1 and FALSE is interpreted as 0.

- You can use a numeric expression in place of a logical one. If the expression evaluates to 0, Excel considers it to be FALSE; any other number is considered to be TRUE.

- For sorting purposes, TRUE is interpreted as 1 and FALSE is interpreted as 0. See "Sorting Data" on page 70.

Comparing Different Data Types

In general, avoid comparing values of different data types. Excel doesn't try to coerce the two values to a common data type. Instead, it evaluates mixed-type comparisons by using a few simple rules:

- Text strings compare greater than numbers and dates. For example, "text" > 5, "5" > 5, and "" > 0 all return TRUE.

- Logical values compare unequally to numbers and dates. For example, TRUE = 1 and FALSE = 0 both return FALSE. TRUE <> 1 returns TRUE.

- Logical values compare unequally to text strings. TRUE = "text" and FALSE = "FALSE" both return FALSE. TRUE <> "TRUE" returns TRUE.

The & Operator

The & (ampersand) operator on the alphabetic or numeric keyboard joins (concatenates) text strings. If A1 contains "aaa", B1 contains "bbb", and C1 contains "ccc", then the formula

    =A1 & B1 & C1

returns "aaabbbccc".

You must add whitespace or delimiters (field separators) between the strings manually:

    =A1 & ", " & B1 & ", " & C1

returns "aaa, bbb, ccc". The constant text values in the preceding formula are surrounded by quotation marks.

As an alternative to the & operator, you can use the CONCATENATE function.

Using comparison operators in formulas

You can use cell references or constants in comparisons. The expression A1=A2, for example, is TRUE if cell A1 contains the same value as cell A2. Comparison operations are used mainly in IF, AND, OR, NOT, XOR, COUNTIF, SUMIF, AVERAGEIF, and other functions that take expressions that can be evaluated as TRUE or FALSE. For example, the formula

    =IF(C2=0,0,C1/C2)

uses a comparison to avoid dividing by zero.

Comparisons don't have to be embedded in functions; you can type them as stand-alone formulas. For example, the formula

    =A1=5

will display TRUE or FALSE in a cell depending on the value in A1. Note that it's clearer to enter this formula as

    =(A1=5)

You can use the alphabetic or numeric keyboard to insert a comparison operator in a formula. (The numeric keyboard provides the quickest access to operators.)

Tip: Excel includes several IS functions that check a specified value and return TRUE or FALSE depending on the outcome. These functions are ISBLANK, ISERR, ISERROR, ISLOGICAL, ISNA, ISNONTEXT, ISNUMBER, ISREF, and ISTEXT. For example, ISBLANK(*value*) returns TRUE if the *value* argument is a reference to an empty cell; otherwise, it returns FALSE.

Functions

Functions are built-in, specialized, named operations that you can use in your formulas. You can combine functions with constants, operators, and cell references to create powerful formulas. Excel provides more than 340 functions, ranging from simple ones that sum or average numbers to complex ones that do financial and engineering calculations. In addition to working with numbers, functions can do calendar arithmetic, make logical decisions, search and transform text, and look up values in lists.

Excel for iPad has a compact help window for every function. For complete documentation, search for the Microsoft support article "Excel functions (by category)" at *support.office.com*. Table 5.6 lists some of the most commonly used functions.

Tip: Excel programmers can create custom functions by using the Visual Basic for Applications (VBA) programming language.

Table 5.6 Commonly Used Excel Functions

Function	Description
ABS	Returns the absolute value of a number.
AND/OR/NOT/XOR	Creates a conditional formula that results in a logical value.
AVERAGE/AVERAGEIF	Calculates the arithmetic mean of a group of numbers.
CONVERT	Converts a number from one measurement system to another.
COUNT/COUNTIF	Counts the number of numbers or dates in a range.
DATE/TIME	Returns the serial number of a specific date or time.
DATEDIF	Calculates the time difference between two dates.
FIND/SEARCH	Finds one text string within another.
FV/NPV/PV	Calculates the future value, net present value, and present value.
IF	Creates a conditional formula that results in another calculation.
INT	Rounds a number down to the nearest integer.
IFERROR/ISERROR/ISERR/	Determines whether a value is an error (page 98). Also IFNA and ISNA.
MID	Returns part of a text string.
MIN/MAX	Returns the smallest and largest value of a group of numbers.
NETWORKDAYS	Calculates the number of working days between two dates.
NOW/TODAY	Returns the current date and time or the current date. See also "Recalculating Manually" on page 72.
PMT	Calculates loan payments.
RAND/RANDBETWEEN	RAND returns a uniform random number between 0 and 1. RANDBETWEEN returns a uniform random integer between specified lower and upper bounds. See also "Recalculating Manually" on page 72.
REPLACE/SUBSTITUTE	Replaces one text string with another.
ROUND	Rounds a number to the specified number of decimal places.
SQRT	Returns a number's square root.
SUM/SUMIF	Sums a group of numbers.
TRIM	Removes extra spaces from text.
UPPER/LOWER/PROPER	Changes the case of text.
VALUE	Converts text to a number.
VLOOKUP/HLOOKUP/LOOKUP	Looks up values in a list.

Function basics

Each function has a name followed by zero or more comma-separated arguments enclosed in parentheses. You use **arguments** to provide the values that the function needs to do its work. The CONVERT function, for example, takes a number in one measurement system and converts it to another system. Its **syntax**—which gives a function's name and the names and order of its arguments—is

CONVERT(*number,from_unit,to_unit*)

Using CONVERT with sample arguments gives the formula

=CONVERT(100,"C","F")

This formula displays 212 in a cell—100 degrees Celsius expressed in the Fahrenheit scale, and

=CONVERT(25,"km","mi")

displays the number of miles in 25 kilometers (15.53427...).

In Figure 5.9, the CONVERT functions in the fourth column get their arguments from the first three columns by using cell references.

The number and types of arguments vary by function. You can type arguments directly into the formula or use cell references for some or all arguments. Arguments can be constants, operator expressions, cell references, or other functions. Surround text arguments with double quotes (but don't put cell references inside double quotes—they aren't considered to be text even if their cells contain text). Here are a few examples of valid arguments:

=CONVERT(60+40,"C","F")

=CONVERT(A2,B2,C2)

=CONVERT(A2+10,B2,UPPER("f"))

=CONVERT(SUM(D2:D10)+SUM(F2:F10)-273.15,B2,UPPER(LEFT("fahrenheit", 1)))

Functions that take no arguments need no user-supplied data to do their work. The TODAY function, for example, returns today's date:

=TODAY()

and the RAND function returns a uniform random number between 0 and 1:

=RAND()

Functions have higher precedence than arithmetic operators and comparison operators. The expression SUM(A2, B2) + 5 > 10, for example, evaluates as ((SUM(A2, B2)) + 5) > 10. See also "Evaluation Order" on page 78.

	A	B	C	D	E	F	G
1	number	from_unit	to_unit	CONVERT			
2	100	C	F	=CONVERT(A2,B2,C2)			
3	25	km	mi	15.53427981			
4	32	F	C	0			
5	100	km	m	100000			
6	1	yr	d	365.25			
7							

Figure 5.9 Example arguments for the CONVERT function.

Inserting functions

A function can be one of several elements in a formula, or it can be the only element in a formula. When you build a formula, you can type the function names manually or use **Formula AutoComplete** to insert them. The Formula AutoComplete menus let you flick through Excel's entire library of functions. When you find the function you want, Excel inserts it into your formula, including argument placeholders (Figure 5.10). Argument placeholders are gray for required arguments and light gray for optional arguments. A selected placeholder is green.

In Figure 5.11, the arguments for the function in cell F2 are all cell references, except for the last argument, which is optional and, here, omitted. The default value of the PV function's optional type argument is 0.

To insert a function in a formula:

1. In the formula bar, position the insertion point where you want the function to appear, or select some text to replace.

2. Do any of the following:
   - On the Formulas tab in the ribbon, tap a function category (Recent, Financial, Logical, and so on) and then tap a function name in the menu.
   - On the left side of the formula bar, tap the Insert Function button fx and then tap a function name in the Functions menu (Figure 5.12).
   - Tap Abc to show the alphabetic keyboard and then type the function name manually. If you're creating a new formula, type = first. As you type, the Functions menu opens to show matching function names. You can tap a name in the menu or keep typing.
   - To get help with a function, tap ⓘ next to its name in a menu. After you finish reading, tap ❮ at the top of the window to return to the menu (Figure 5.13). The help window includes a function's name, purpose, and syntax.

Excel inserts the function and its argument placeholders in the formula bar. (If you typed the entire function name manually, Excel doesn't insert argument placeholders.)

Figure 5.10 Formula AutoComplete inserts a function and placeholders for its arguments.

	A	B	C	D	E	F	G
	fx	=PV(A2,B2,C2,D2)					
1	rate	nper	pmt	fv	type	PV	
2	0.25%	180	($100.00)	$100,000.00		($49,318.08)	
3	0.25%	180	($100.00)	$100,000.00	0	($49,318.08)	
4	0.25%	180	($100.00)	$100,000.00	1	($49,281.88)	
5							

Figure 5.11 Here, the function arguments are cell references, as shown in the formula bar.

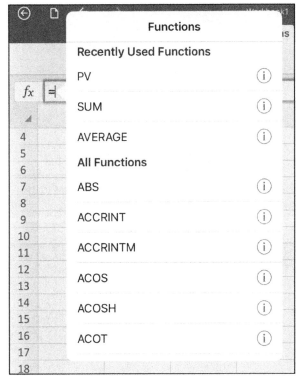

Figure 5.12 Tap a function in the Functions menu to insert it in a formula.

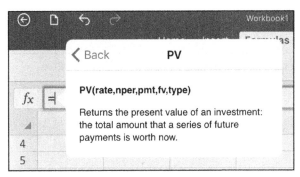

Figure 5.13 The help window for a function.

3. In the formula bar, tap each argument placeholder and then do any of the following:

   ▸ Tap a cell or drag across a cell range to insert a cell reference.

   ▸ Type the name of a cell reference.

   ▸ Type an argument manually on the keyboard.

   ▸ Insert a nested function by using any of the methods described in the preceding step.

   ▸ To omit an optional argument (indicated by a dimmed placeholder), leave its placeholder as is. Excel deletes the placeholder when you save the formula.

Optional Arguments

Some functions take **optional arguments**. If you omit an optional argument from the function, Excel uses a **default value** when it evaluates the function. If you want to use a value other than the default, specify an optional argument just as you would a required one. The LOG function, for example, returns the logarithm of a positive number by using a specified base. LOG has two arguments:

   LOG(*number,base*)

The first argument is required; the second is optional. (Optional arguments, if they exist, always follow required ones.) If you omit *base*, it is assumed to be 10. Hence

   =LOG(100)

is the same as

   =LOG(100,10)

When you insert a function in the formula bar, the placeholders for optional arguments are dimmed (light gray). If you omit some optional arguments but not others, don't delete the commas between them.

AutoSum

People so often sum a row or column of values that Excel has a feature dedicated to that purpose: the **AutoSum** button on the Formulas tab. The button has a picture of the Greek letter Σ (uppercase sigma), which means *sum* to mathematicians.

When you tap the AutoSum button, Excel makes an educated guess about which cells you want to total. If you're at the end of a row, for example, Excel assumes you want to add all the numeric values in all the columns on the left. If you're at the bottom of a column of numbers, Excel assumes you want to add the values above. If you select multiple cells along the edge of a range of rows or columns, AutoSum inserts multiple formulas.

When you tap the AutoSum button, Excel creates a formula with the cell range it thinks you need, and highlights the cells in a marquee box (Figure 5.14). At this point, you can tap ✓ to accept the formula as-is, type in a new reference, or resize the range by dragging the selection handle.

The AutoSum feature isn't just for summing. You can also use it to calculate averages, counts, maximums, and minimums. To do so, tap the AutoSum button and then tap the calculation option in the AutoSum Functions menu (Figure 5.15). Excel inserts the appropriate function into the cell and guesses which nearby cells to use for the calculation.

Tip: You can also tap the Σ key on the numeric keyboard to invoke AutoSum, but you get only SUM formulas—other calculations aren't available.

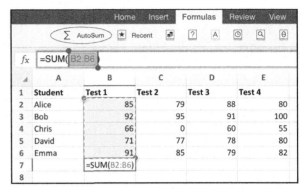

Figure 5.14 AutoSum guesses which nearby cells to use for the calculation.

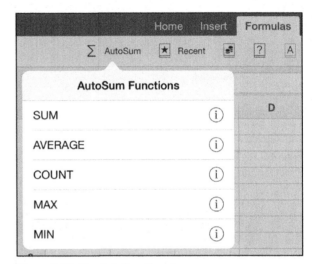

Figure 5.15 The AutoSum Functions menu.

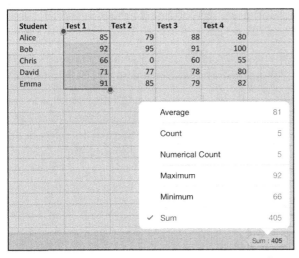

Figure 5.16 Tap the summary label to view statistics for the current selection.

Summary calculations without formulas

Excel provides a handy calculation tool in the bottom-right corner of the screen. Select one or more cells and then look down at the summary label; you'll see the sum of values that you selected.

To choose which calculation is displayed, tap the summary label and then, in the menu that appears, tap one of the following options (Figure 5.16):

- **Average.** The average (arithmetic mean) of the selected numbers or dates.

- **Count.** The number of selected cells that contain some type of content (that is, cells that aren't empty).

- **Numerical Count.** The number of selected cells that contain numbers or dates.

- **Maximum.** The selected number or date with the largest value (for dates, this means the latest date).

- **Minimum.** The selected number or date with the smallest value (for dates, this means the earliest date).

- **Sum.** The sum of all selected numbers. Although you can use Sum with date values, totaling dates generates meaningless results.

Tip: If you select cells that have a mix of date and numeric values, most of the summary calculations won't work properly because Excel stores date values as numbers internally. Combining date numbers and real numbers yields a meaningless result.

Chapter 5　Formulas and Functions　93

Copying and Moving Formulas

When you copy or move cells containing constants such as numbers, text, dates, or logical values, Excel duplicates the values in the target cells. Copying and moving formulas, however, is complicated by cell references, which you may not want to duplicate. Excel's default behavior is what you want most of the time:

- When you *move* a formula cell, Excel leaves its original cell references untouched; in its new location, the formula still points to the same cells that it used to.

- When you *copy* a formula cell, Excel updates the formula's cell references so that they point to different cells relative to the formula's new location.

In Figure 5.17, the original formula, in cell C1, sums cells A1 and B1.

When you *move* C1 to C2, the cell references don't change: the formula still sums A1 and B1 (Figure 5.18).

When you *copy* C1 to C2 and C3, the cell references change: each copied formula sums the two cells to its left—the same relative position of the referenced cells in the original formula (Figure 5.19).

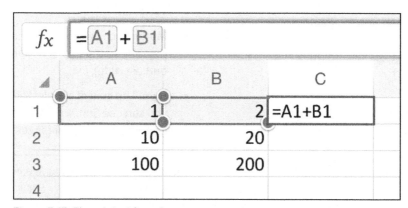

Figure 5.17 The original formula.

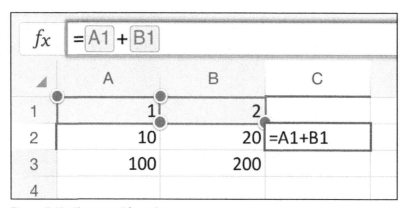

Figure 5.18 The moved formula.

You can move formulas by dragging. You can copy formulas by cut-and-paste, copy-and-paste, or filling. These techniques are covered in "Cutting, Copying, and Pasting Cells" on page 64 and "Filling Cells with Data Series" on page 68. You might think that cut-and-paste moves a cell, but it actually copies it—it only looks moved because its contents disappear from its original location. Excel considers all pasted cells to be copies of the original.

Excel pastes formulas by default but gives you the option to paste values instead. To choose a paste option, tap 📋 near the pasted cells (this icon appears right after you paste). Tapping Paste Values in the 📋 menu pastes the computed result of the formula but not the actual formula—which is handy when you have a result that you no longer want to update (Figure 5.20).

To copy the *text* of a formula, double-tap an empty area in the formula bar and then tap Select All on the pop-up menu. (To copy only part of the text, drag the selection handles ● to encompass the characters that you want to copy.) Tap Copy on the pop-up menu. When you paste the formula's text in a new cell, all the cell references stay the same as they were in the original.

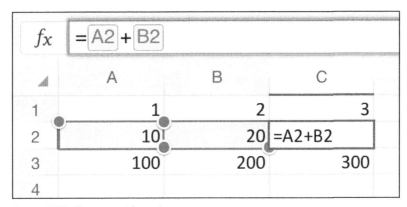

Figure 5.19 The copied formula.

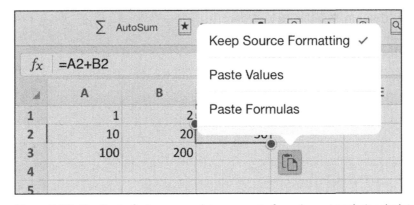

Figure 5.20 The Paste Options menu lets you paste formulas or just their calculated values.

Chapter 5 Formulas and Functions 95

Relative vs. absolute cell references

By default, cell addresses in formulas are **relative cell references**, meaning their row or column addresses can change when you copy formulas. For situations where you want to preserve row or column positions, Excel offers **absolute cell references**, which freeze cell addresses no matter where you copy formula cells.

To set relative and absolute cell references:

1. Double-tap the cell containing the formula that you want to change.

2. In the formula bar, tap or move the insertion point next to the placeholder of the target cell reference, and then tap References Types on the pop-up menu (Figure 5.21).

3. In the Cell Reference Types menu, tap one of the following options (Figure 5.22). A $ character in the cell reference indicates an absolute row or column.

   - **A1: Relative Column, Relative Row.** When the formula cell is copied, the cell reference changes so that it retains the same position relative to the formula cell.

   - **A1: Absolute Column, Absolute Row.** When the formula cell is copied, the cell reference doesn't change.

   - **A$1: Relative Column, Absolute Row.** When the formula cell is copied, only the column component can change to retain its position relative to the formula cell.

   - **$A1: Absolute Column, Relative Row.** When the formula cell is copied, only the row component can change to retain its position relative to the formula cell.

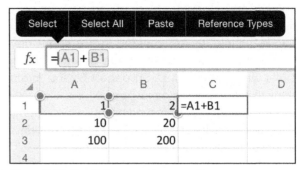

Figure 5.21 Tap References Types on the pop-up menu.

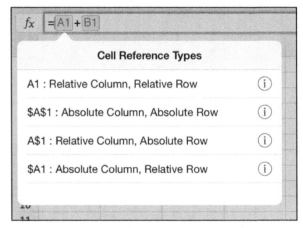

Figure 5.22 The Cell Reference Types menu.

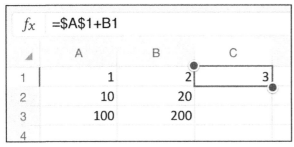

Figure 5.23 A cell with mixed relative and absolute references.

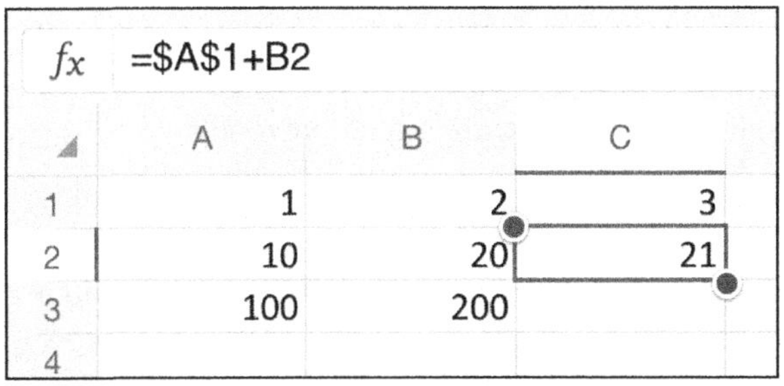

In Figure 5.23, the formula in cell C1 sums cells A1 and B1, but uses the absolute cell reference A1. The B1 reference is relative.

When this formula is copied to cell C2 (Figure 5.24), the B1 reference changes to B2, but A1 stays anchored.

Figure 5.24 The copied cell retains its absolute reference but not its relative reference.

Correcting Common Formula Errors

If you make a syntax error when entering a formula (like omitting a function argument or including a mismatched number of parentheses), Excel opens a message box and won't accept the formula until you fix it.

It's also possible, though, to write a legitimate formula that doesn't return a valid answer. For example, the formula

=A1/A2

works fine if cells A1 and A2 both contain numbers (and A2 is nonzero). But if A2 is empty or zero, or if A1 or A2 contains text, then Excel can't evaluate the formula and displays an error value in the cell.

Excel's **error values**, which all begin with a # symbol, are listed in Table 5.7. To continue working, you must track down the problem and resolve it, which may mean correcting the formula or changing the cells that it references.

Unfortunately, Excel for iPad lacks the formula-auditing tools of Excel for Windows or Mac, but you can create error-trapping formulas by using the IFERROR, IFNA, ISERR, ISERROR, ISNA, NA, and ERROR.TYPE functions.

Tip: If an entire cell is filled with # symbols, then the column isn't wide enough to display the value. You can either widen the column or change the number format of the cell.

Circular References

One of the most common (and annoying) errors is the **circular reference**, which occurs when you create a formula that depends, indirectly or directly, on its own value. If you enter the formula

=A1+1

in cell A1, for example, then Excel must take the current value of A1 and add 1. This operation changes the value of A1, however, forcing Excel to calculate the formula all over again. If unchecked, this process would continue endlessly, never producing a final result.

Circular references typically are easy to identify and fix. But when a circular reference is indirect (as when a formula refers to another formula that refers to yet another formula that refers back to the original formula), some detective work may be needed to solve the problem.

Excel for iPad doesn't allow circular references. When you enter a formula that contains a circular reference, Excel opens a message box and makes you fix the formula by removing the reference.

Tip: Excel for Windows and Mac allow circular references if you enable iterative calculation in the Formulas section of the Excel Options or Preferences dialog box. Excel for iPad doesn't support this setting, however.

Table 5.7 Excel Error Values

Error Value	Description
#DIV/0	The formula is trying to divide by zero. This error also occurs if you try to divide by a cell that's empty, because Excel treats an empty cell as though it contains the number 0 in simple calculations with arithmetic operators. (Some functions, like AVERAGE, ignore empty cells.)
#NAME?	The formula uses a name that Excel doesn't recognize. This error usually occurs when you misspell a range name or function name, enter text with missing or mismatched quotes, or omit the empty parentheses after a function name.
#N/A	The formula refers (directly or indirectly) to a cell that uses the NA function to signal that data is not available. Some functions (VLOOKUP and some statistical functions, for example) can also return #N/A.
#NULL!	The formula uses an intersection of two ranges that don't intersect. Recall that the intersection operator finds cells that two ranges have in common. This error occurs when there are no cells in common. You may have used the intersection operator by accident, as the operator is only a single-space character.
#NUM!	A problem with a number exists. This error often occurs when a calculation produces a number that's too large (overflow) or too small (underflow) for Excel to handle, or when a formula tries to calculate the square root of a negative number or the log of a nonpositive number.
#REF!	The formula refers to a cell that isn't valid. This error can occur when you delete or paste over cells that a formula is using, copy a formula from one worksheet to another, or hide the Total row (page 110) of a table.
#VALUE!	The formula uses the wrong type of data. This error can occur when you use arithmetic operators with text instead of numbers. Or when you refer to a range of cells when a function argument expects a single value.

CHAPTER 6

Tables

A common way to organize data in a worksheet is in a structured list, also called a table. A table is a rectangular range of data that usually has a row of text headings that describe the contents of each column. Excel's table feature makes common tasks much easier and helps eliminate some common errors.

Tip: Don't confuse structured tables with the variable data tables used for what-if analysis. These tables have a similar name but nothing else in common.

Excel Tables vs. Databases

If you've worked with a relational database system such as Oracle or Microsoft Access, then you're familiar with some of Excel's table concepts—namely, the idea of columns (fields) and rows (records). Databases and Excel tables are two very different creatures, however.

- Databases tables have much stricter rules than Excel tables. Before you can add any data to a database table, you must define the table and its primary and foreign keys; specify each column's name, data type, and range of acceptable values; set user permissions; and so on. Excel provides some data-validation features, but they're optional and not especially rigid.

- Databases are **relational**, meaning they contain multiple tables that can be linked to one another. A relational database might link customers in one table to their orders in another, for example. An Excel workbook can hold multiple tables, but it's a chore to combine their data.

- Databases play a dramatically different role than spreadsheets. Excel is typically an end-user program, whereas massive and powerful databases are designed and maintained by full-time administrators, and are crucial for keeping an organization running.

Table Basics

A **table** is a rectangular range that contains structured data about a specific entity type. Because table data is structured, the rules for columns and rows are stricter for tables than for ordinary ranges.

- A table's **entity type** is a class of distinguishable real-world objects, events, or concepts with common properties. Examples of entity types include employees, customers, bank transactions, products, appointments, patients, movies, genes, weather conditions, invoices, and projects.

- Each row in the table corresponds to a single **entity**, which is a unique instance of an entity type. For example, a row can contain information about a particular employee, customer, bank transaction, product, and so on.

- Each column contains a specific attribute (or property) about the table's entity type. For example, if each row contains information about an employee, the columns can contain data such as name, employee number, hire date, salary, department, and so on. Tables typically have a **header row** at the top that contains the name of each column.

Setting up data in a rectangular range of cells is straightforward, as is converting that range to a table. Excel responds intelligently to actions that you perform with a table. If you create a chart from a table, for example, the chart will expand automatically as you add or delete rows in the table. And if you enter a formula in a table cell, Excel propagates that formula to other rows in the same column of the table.

Figure 6.1 shows the main parts of a table. A table differs from a standard range in that, with a table:

- When you select a cell in a table, you can use the commands on the Table contextual tab in the ribbon (Figure 6.2).

- The cells have consistent background and text colors.

- Each **column header** has a drop-down list that lets you sort the data or filter the table to display only rows that meet certain criteria.

- If the active cell is within the table, when you scroll down the worksheet so that the header row disappears, the column headers replace the column letters in the worksheet header.

- Tables support calculated columns. A single formula entered in any row in a column propagates to all cells in the column automatically.

- Tables support structured references. Instead of using cell references, formulas in tables can use column names (page 113).

- Near the bottom-right corner of a table is a control that you can drag to resize the table, adding more columns or rows.

- Near the top-left corner of a table is a control that you can tap to select the entire table or drag to move the table.

- Selecting rows and columns within the table is simplified.

Sort and filter controls in the header row (A1:E1)

The entire table (A1:E17)   The table data (A2:E16)   A column and column header (D1:D17)   A calculated column (E1:E17)

	A	B	C	D	E
1	Salesperson ▼	Region ▼	Sales ▼	CommissionRate ▼	Commission ▼
2	Michael	East	$400	20%	$80
3	Barbara	South	$170	15%	$26
4	Richard	West	$170	10%	$17
5	Robert	North	$830	15%	$125
6	Maria	East	$460	10%	$46
7	John	North	$480	10%	$48
8	Susan	East	$460	15%	$69
9	Charles	East	$390	20%	$78
10	Dorothy	South	$820	15%	$123
11	Joseph	East	$270	10%	$27
12	William	South	$320	20%	$64
13	David	North	$410	15%	$62
14	Patricia	North	$670	10%	$67
15	Margaret	North	$840	15%	$126
16	Mary	East	$340	15%	$51
17	Total		15	$7,030	14%	$1,008
18					

The Total row (A17:E17)

Figure 6.1 The parts of a table.

Figure 6.2 The Table tab appears in the ribbon when any cell in a table is selected.

Chapter 6 Tables   103

Creating a Table

Most of the time, you'll create a table from an existing range of data (specifically, a rectangular range of structured data with column headers). Excel also lets you create a table from an empty range, so that you can fill in the details later. A few tips before you start:

- If you're creating a new table, the worksheet's first row is a good place to begin. (You can always shift the table down later by selecting a cell in the top row and then choosing Home tab > Insert Sheet Rows.) This first row of the table is where you enter the column headers.

- If necessary, rearrange your worksheet so that the table data is separated from any other (nontable) data by at least one empty row and column. Excel needs an empty buffer around the range to guess a table's dimensions correctly.

- Don't put (nontable) data in the cells *below* your table. If your table expands too far down, you'll run up against these filled-in cells. You can always use commands like Home tab > Insert Sheet Rows to insert extra space, but it's better to anticipate problems rather than react to them. Some Excel pros never put *any* nontable data in a worksheet that contains a table, reasoning that it will just get in the way as the table grows or shrinks over time. Even so, Excel makes an effort to leave the rest of your worksheet alone when you change your table's structure. When you expand a table vertically or horizontally, for example, Excel moves cells out of the way only when it absolutely needs more space.

- Choose column headers carefully, as they are the basis for all the searching, sorting, and filtering you'll do later. If you're building a table of names and addresses, for example, don't combine First Name and Last Name into a single column, or you won't be able to sort by Last Name. In general, use columns whose values can't be meaningfully subdivided.

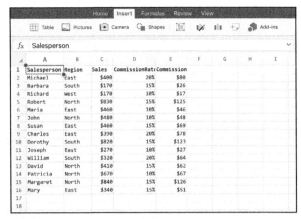

Figure 6.3 A range of structured data ready to be converted to a table.

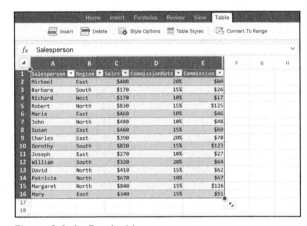

Figure 6.4 An Excel table.

104   Excel for iPad & iPad Pro

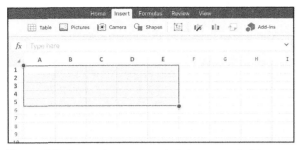

Figure 6.5 An empty range ready to be converted to a table.

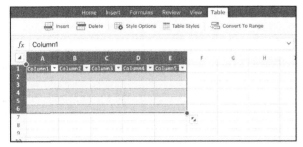

Figure 6.6 An empty table.

To create a table from existing data:

1 Make sure that the range doesn't contain any completely blank rows or columns; otherwise, Excel won't guess the table range correctly.

2 Select any cell within the range (Figure 6.3).

3 Tap Table on the Insert tab.

Excel converts the range to a table and the Table tab appears in the ribbon (Figure 6.4).

To create a table from an empty range:

1 Select the empty range (Figure 6.5).

2 Tap Table on the Insert tab.

Excel converts the range to a table and the Table tab appears in the ribbon (Figure 6.6).

3 Replace the generic column headers (Column1, Column2, and so on) with meaningful names.

Formatting a Table

When you create a table, Excel applies the default table style. The actual appearance depends on which template (page 31) was used to create the workbook. If you prefer a different look, you can change the style of the table. A **table style** is a collection of formatting settings that applies to an entire table. If you add new rows to a table, Excel applies consistent cell formatting automatically. Or, if you delete rows, Excel adjusts the formatting of all the cells underneath to make sure that the **banding** (the alternating pattern of cell shading that makes each row easier to read) stays consistent.

Tip: Table styles don't change the fonts in a table.

To change the style of a table:

1. Select any cell in the table.
2. Tap Table tab > Table Styles and then tap a style in the menu (Figure 6.7).

   Excel applies the style to the entire table.

Tip: If a table style doesn't work, it's probably because the range was already formatted before you converted it to a table. Table styles don't override manual formatting. To clear existing formatting, select the entire table, tap the Home tab, set the background color to No Fill, set the font color to Automatic, and set the cell borders to No Border. Now table styles should work as expected.

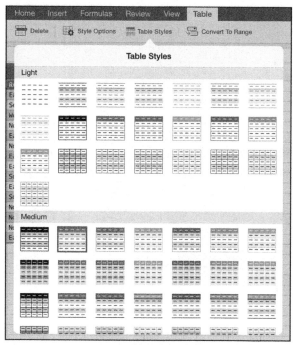

Figure 6.7 The Table Styles menu.

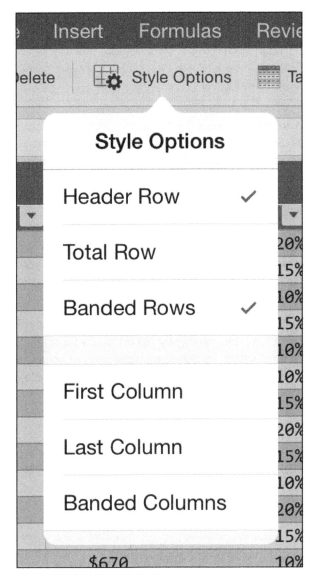

Figure 6.8 The Table Style Options menu.

Along with table styles, you have a few more options to fine-tune a table's appearance. The Table Style Options menu lets you toggle on or off different table elements.

To choose style options for a table:

1. Select any cell in the table.
2. Tap Table tab > Style Options (Figure 6.8).
3. Toggle any of the following options.

   ▸ **Header Row** lets you show or hide the row with column titles at the top of the table. You'll rarely want to turn off this option. Column headers are informative and include drop-down lists for sorting and filtering the table.

   ▸ **Total Row** lets you show or hide the row that displays summary calculations at the bottom of the table. See "Using the Total Row" on page 110.

   ▸ **Banded Row** applies different formatting to every other row, if it's defined in the table style. Usually, the banded row appears with a background fill. Banding makes it easier to scan across a row without losing your place.

   ▸ **First Column** applies different formatting to the first column in the table, if it's defined in the table style.

   ▸ **Last Column** applies different formatting to the last column in the table, if it's defined in the table style.

   ▸ **Banded Column** applies different formatting to every other column, if it's defined in the table style. Banded columns are less useful than banded rows, because people usually read tables from side to side, not top to bottom.

Working with a Table

Excel offers time-saving ways to navigate in a table, select parts of a table, edit table rows and columns, and more (Figure 6.9).

Navigating in a table. Selecting cells in a table works like selecting cells in a normal range. One difference is when you use the Tab key on the numeric keyboard. Tapping Tab moves to the cell to the right, but when you reach the last column, tapping Tab again moves to the first cell in the next row.

Selecting an entire column. In the table, tap any cell in the column that you want to select, and then tap that column's heading at the top of the worksheet (that's the *worksheet's* column heading you tap, not the *table's* column heading). Excel selects the column's cells within the table. To extend the selection to multiple columns, drag the selection handles ● left or right.

Selecting an entire row. In the table, tap any cell in the row that you want to select, and then tap that row's heading on the left edge of the worksheet. Excel selects the row's cells within the table. To extend the selection to multiple rows, drag the selection handles ● up or down.

Selecting an entire table. Select any cell in the table and then tap ◢ near the top-left corner of the table. You can also select a table manually by dragging from the table's top-left cell to its bottom-right cell. If the table's top-left corner is cell A1, tap ◢ twice to select the entire table (tapping only once selects the entire *worksheet*).

Adding new rows. Select any cell in the table. Near the bottom-right corner of the table, drag ◤ down to add new rows. Similarly, if you enter data in the row just below the last row in the table, the table extends down automatically to include the new row. To insert a row anywhere in the table, select a cell where you want to insert the row. To insert multiple rows, select a range of cells. Then tap Table tab > Insert > Table Rows Above (or tap Insert > Rows Above on the pop-up menu).

Tip: An exception to extending tables automatically is when the table is displaying a Total row (page 110). If you enter data below the Total row, the table won't be extended to include the new data.

Adding new columns. Select any cell in the table. Near the bottom-right corner of the table, drag ◤ right to add new columns. Similarly, if you enter data in the column to the right of the last column in the table, the table extends right automatically to include the new column. To insert a column anywhere in the table, select a cell where you want to insert the column. To insert multiple columns, select a range of cells. Then tap Table tab > Insert > Table Columns Left (or tap Insert > Columns Left on the pop-up menu).

Deleting rows or columns. To delete a row (or column) in a table, select any cell in the row (or column) to be deleted. To delete multiple rows or columns, select a range of cells. Then tap Table tab > Delete > Table Rows (or Delete > Table Columns). Similarly, you can select table rows or columns and then tap Delete on the pop-up menu.

Tip: When you add or remove rows, you're inserting or deleting *table* rows, not *worksheet* rows. If you have a table with three columns and you delete a row, for example, Excel removes three cells, and then shifts up any table rows underneath. But any data in the same row that exists *outside* the table (say, in the columns to the right of it) is unaffected.

Moving an entire table. Select any cell in the table. Near the top-left corner of the table, drag ◢ to a new location. To move a table to a different worksheet, tap ◢ to select the entire table, tap Cut on the pop-up menu, switch to the target worksheet, and then paste the table.

Converting a table back to a range. If you need to convert a table back to a normal range, select any cell in the table and then tap Table tab > Convert to Range. The table style formatting remains intact, but the range no longer acts like a table.

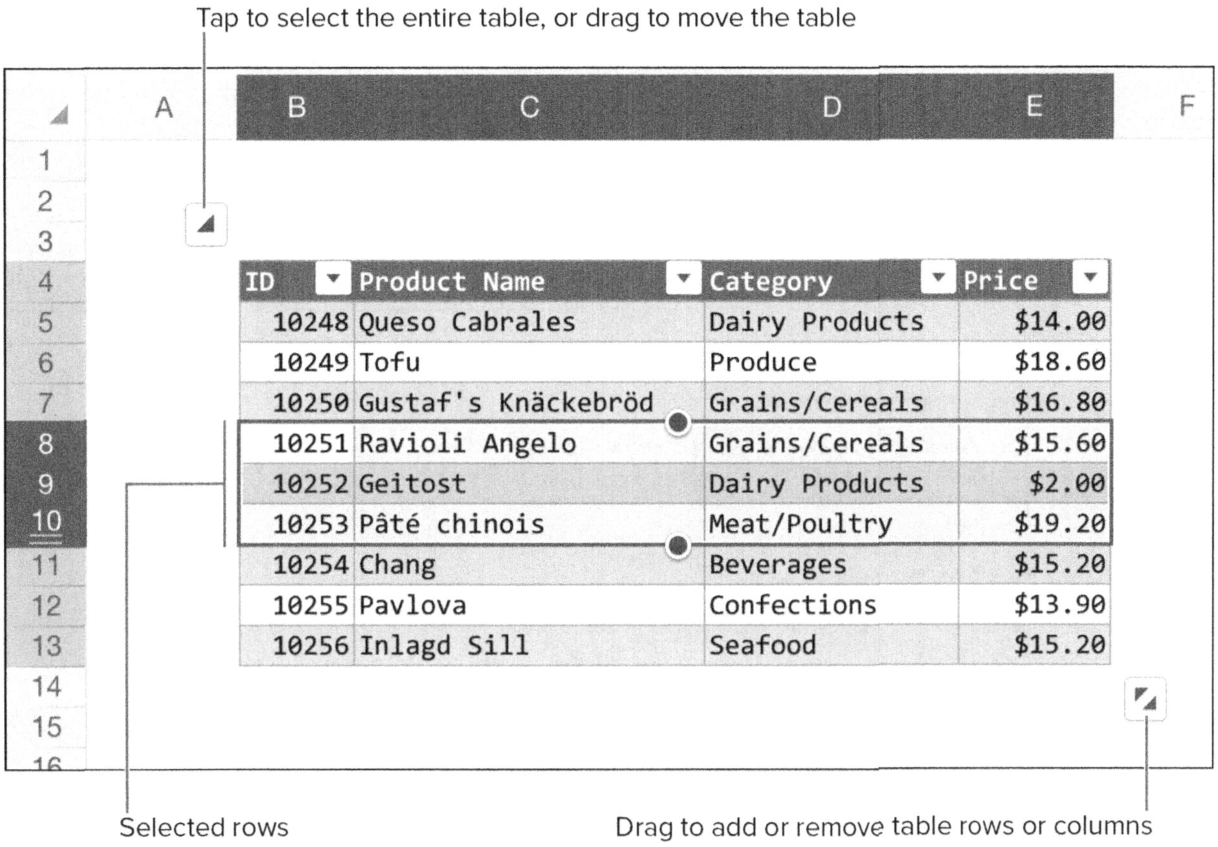

Figure 6.9 When you select a cell in a table, controls appear near the table's top-left and bottom-right corners.

Using the Total Row

Tables make it easy to calculate totals, counts, averages, standard deviations, and other common statistics by using a dedicated summary row. To show this row, select any cell in the table and then turn on Table tab > Style Options > Total Row. Excel adds an extra row at the bottom of the table.

The Total row contains formulas that summarize the values in the columns. By default, the Total row displays the sum of the values in a column of numbers. To show a different summary formula, select a cell in the Total row and then tap ⌄ next to the cell. Select a function in the list or tap More Functions to use a different formula (Figure 6.10).

The Total row uses only the rows that are currently visible, ignoring all filtered rows. This behavior is useful if you want to calculate statistics for a subset of a table's data. If you want to create grand totals that include everything, however, you can write your own summary formula using functions like SUM, COUNT, or AVERAGE. The formulas in the Total row use the SUBTOTAL function to do calculations, which is the only Excel function that takes table filtering into account.

When the Total row is showing, you can't add a new row to the table by typing in the row just below it. Instead, you can add a new row by selecting any cell in the Total row and then choosing Table tab > Insert > Table Rows Above (or tapping Insert > Rows Above on the pop-up menu). Or, if your table has no filtering applied, you can add a row by selecting the cell in the bottom-right corner of the table and then tapping the Tab key.

Tip: If you use a formula that refers to a value in the Total row of a table, the formula returns a #REF! error if you hide the Total row. Unhide the Total row to make the formula work normally.

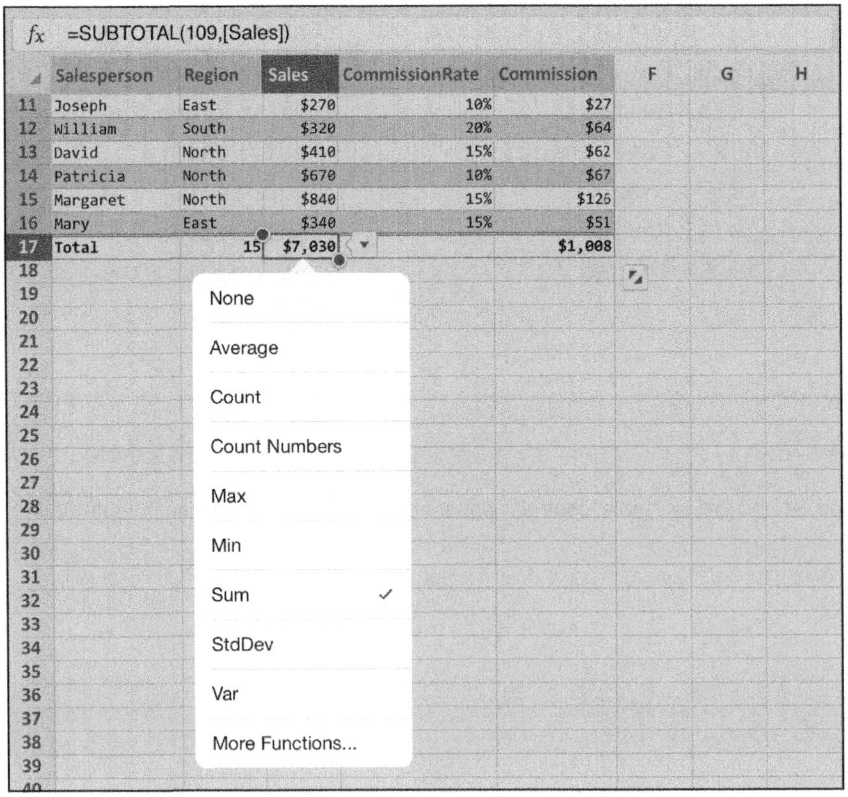

Figure 6.10 The Total row in a table.

Sorting a Table

Sorting a table reorders its rows based on the contents of a particular column. You can sort a table to put names in alphabetical order, for example, or sort salespeople by the total sales made.

To sort a table by a particular column, tap the dropdown arrow ▼ in the column header and then tap one of the sort commands (Figure 6.11). You can sort in ascending order (A, B, C…1, 2, 3…Jan, Feb, Mar) or descending order (Z, Y, X…3, 2, 1…Dec, Nov, Oct).

Tip: To show or hide the sort and filter icons in column headers, select any cell in the table and then tap Home tab > Sort and Filter ᴬ/ᵤ ▽ > Filter.

When you choose a sort option, Excel reorders the rows and places a ↑ or ↓ icon in the column header to indicate the sort direction. Excel doesn't keep re-sorting your data when you edit cells or add new rows. If you make changes and want to reapply the sort, tap the icon in the column header and then choose the same sort option again.

Tip: To sort by more than one column at a time, see "Multicolumn sorts" on page 70.

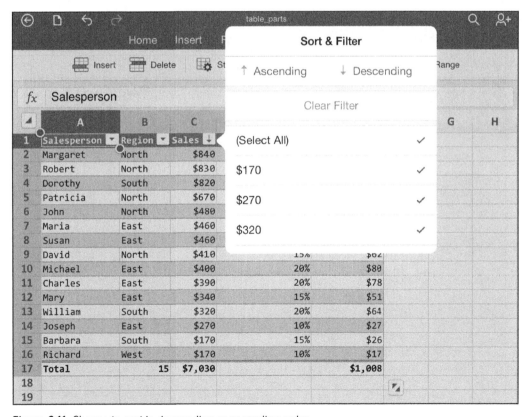

Figure 6.11 Choose to sort in descending or ascending order.

Filtering a Table

Filtering lets you limit the data a table displays so you see only the rows that meet certain conditions (the other rows are hidden). Filtering lets you do things like:

- Show only customers who live in a specific city
- List accounts that currently have a balance due
- Calculate sums and averages for certain products

You can use the Total row (page 110) or the SUB-TOTAL function to do calculations using only cells that are currently visible.

Tip: Filtering hides entire worksheet rows, not just table rows. If you have other data in the filtered rows to the left or right of the table, that data will also be hidden.

Filtering, like sorting, uses the drop-down column headers at the top of a table. When you tap a drop-down arrow , Excel shows a list of all the distinct values in that column (Figure 6.12). Initially, each value has a checkmark next to it. Clear the checkmark to hide rows with that value. To hide all but a few items, clear the Select All checkmark to remove all the checkmarks, and then choose just the rows that you want to see in the table. When you filter on a column, Excel places a filter icon in that column's header. You can filter a table using any number of columns.

Tip: To show or hide the sort and filter icons in column headers, select any cell in the table and then tap Home tab > Sort and Filter > Filter.

When a table is filtered, thick bars in the row headings indicate which row numbers are hidden.

To remove a filter, open the drop-down column menu and then tap Clear Filter.

Tip: When you copy a range from a filtered table, only the visible cells are copied, making it easy to copy a subset of a larger table and paste it elsewhere. The pasted data is just a normal range, not a table, but you can convert the copied range to a table.

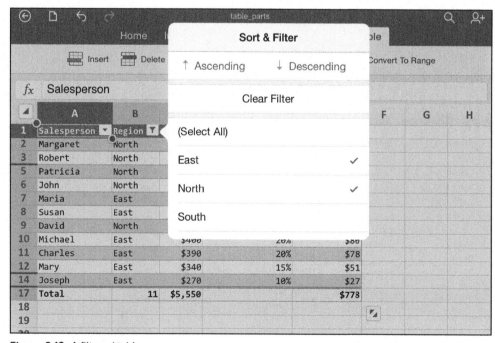

Figure 6.12 A filtered table.

112   Excel for iPad & iPad Pro

Using Formulas in a Table

Excel has several features that help you do calculations on the data inside a table.

Propagating formulas

If you enter or edit a formula in a table cell, Excel propagates that formula to every other row in the same column automatically, no copying and pasting required.

Dynamic calculations

Excel adjusts formulas automatically as a table grows or shrinks. Suppose a table occupies five rows in the range A1:C5. The first row contains column headers, followed by four data rows. You create the following formula to sum the values in the third column:

=SUM(C2:C5)

If you add a new row to the table, Excel updates the formula automatically to include this new row:

=SUM(C2:C6)

The same thing happens if you delete a row, provided the formula references the entire column in the table. The following formula, for example, omits the first row in the table:

=SUM(C3:C5)

If you expand the table now, Excel won't update the formula. You can avoid this problem by using column names (discussed next) in table formulas.

Column names

Excel automatically creates **column names** that you can use when you write formulas inside a table. Each column name is whatever text is in that column's header row. Instead of referring to a specific cell in a formula, you can use the name of the column preceded by an *at symbol* (@) and inside square brackets. If column C in a table is named Price, for example, then the formula:

=C2*0.1

can instead be written as:

=[@Price]*0.1

The @ symbol means "the current row", so [@Price] automatically refers to the value of the Price column in the current row, regardless of the formula's location in the table.

Tip: To type square brackets on the numeric keyboard, touch and hold the parentheses "(" and ")" keys.

It's good practice to always use the @ symbol before a column name. It's not required, though, so the preceding formula is equivalent to:

=[Price]*0.1

If a column name has a space in it, a second set of square brackets around the name is required. To refer to the Tax Rate column in the current row, for example, type:

[@[Tax Rate]]

Column names save time, make worksheets easier to understand, and reduce the likelihood of errors. The purpose of this formula, for example, is immediately clear:

=[@Price] * [@[Tax Rate]] + [@[Shipping Charge]]

Tip: Column names and @ notation are part of the larger topic of **structured references**, which lets you create complex, auto-adjusting formulas that reference all or part of a table. For details, search for the Microsoft support article "Use structured references in Excel table formulas" at *support.office.com*.

CHAPTER 7

Charts

Trends and comparisons are hard to discern from raw data, so Excel provides charts to reveal relationships that aren't apparent by staring at rows and columns of numbers. You can choose from many types of charts—column charts, pie charts, scatter charts, and more—and you can apply different styles, colors, and layouts to customize them. Knowing which chart type to pick isn't always easy, and decorating charts with unnecessary text, lines, and effects will obscure your message.

Chart Basics

The figure below shows the main parts of a chart, which are described in this section.

Chart area

The **chart area** is the entire chart and all its elements. You can tap the chart area to select a chart and open its pop-up menu, drag a chart to move it, or resize a chart by dragging a selection handle on the border of the chart area.

Chart data

To create a chart, you must select at least one cell in a range of data (a set of cells). If you don't want to include specific rows or columns of data in a chart, you can hide them in the worksheet (page 49) or filter them in a table (page 112).

A chart is linked dynamically to its data—when you change a cell's value or select a different range of cells, the associated chart updates automatically. A range can feed data to multiple charts, and a chart can get data from more than one range.

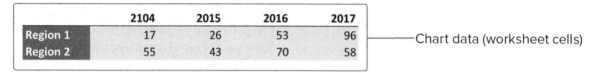
Chart data (worksheet cells)

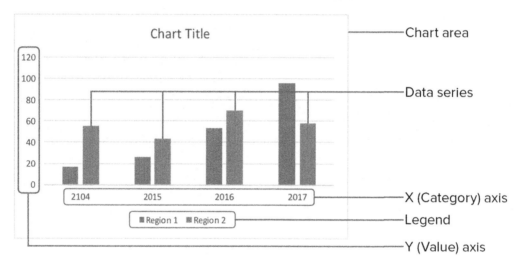
Chart area
Data series
X (Category) axis
Legend
Y (Value) axis

Excel can recommend charts for you. The charts that it suggests depend on how you've arranged the data in your worksheet. You may also have specific charts in mind. Either way, the best ways to arrange your data for a given chart are:

- For column, bar, line, area, surface, and radar charts, arrange the data in columns and rows.

Lorem	Ipsum
1	2
3	4

Lorem	1	3
Ipsum	2	4

- For pie charts, arrange the data in one column or row, and one column or row of labels. A pie chart uses one data series.

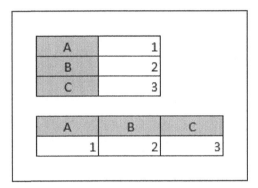

- For doughnut charts, arrange the data in multiple columns or rows, and one column or row of labels. A doughnut chart can use one or more data series.

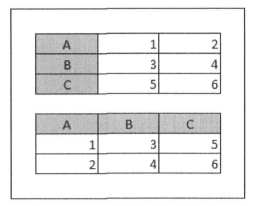

- For scatter (XY) and bubble charts, arrange the data in columns, placing the x values in the first column and the y values and bubble sizes in the next two columns. Scatter and bubble charts can use one or more data series.

X	Y	Bubble size
1	2	3
4	5	6

- For stock charts, arrange the data in columns or rows, using a combination of volume, open, high, low, and close values, with names or dates as labels in the correct order.

Date	High	Low	Close
1/1/2014	46.125	42.012	44.063

Date	1/1/2014
High	46.125
Low	42.012
Close	44.063

Data points and data series

The data for the column chart in the following figure has eight **data points** (individual values)—four for each region. Region 1 and Region 2 are called the **data series** because each region's data points appear as a series of columns of the same color, one column for each year. Each Region 1 column is paired beside its corresponding Region 2 column, and each side-by-side set of columns is called a **category** (2014 is a category, 2015 is a category, and so on).

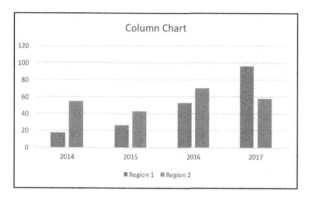

Excel lets you switch (transpose) data series to change the emphasis of your data. In the following figure, data points are grouped by region rather than by year. The chart contains two sets of four columns (eight data points). The data points for each year are data series (each series has only two data points) and each region is a category.

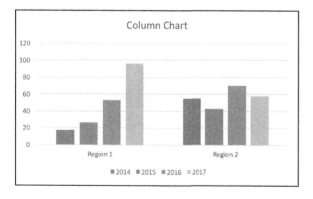

Legend

The **legend** shows the colors, symbols, and labels used for each data series in the chart. The legend's labels come from the row or column headers in the chart data. Some chart layouts let you hide the legend.

X axis and y axis

The **x axis** and the **y axis** are the horizontal and vertical lines that give a chart scale and context. In column, line, bar, and area charts, data points are plotted on one axis (the y axis for column, line, and area charts; the x axis for bar charts) and categories are grouped on the other axis. The data-point (numeric) axis is called the **value axis**, and the data-set (group) axis is called the **category axis**. In scatter charts, both the x and y axes are value axes. Pie charts have no axes. Category axes are labeled with text from row or column headers in the chart data; value axes are labeled with a numeric range. Axes are marked by stepped graduations called **gridlines**.

Picking a Chart Type

Excel offers different chart types, each of which is designed for certain situations or data types. Each chart type has its strengths and weaknesses for different types of data.

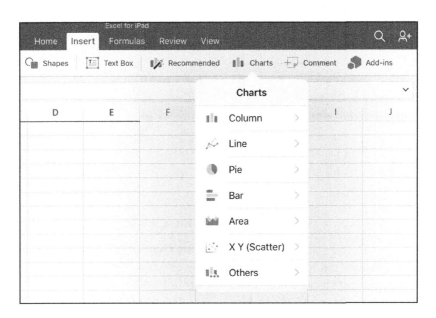

Column charts

Column charts, also called clustered column charts, display vertical columns with lengths proportional to the values that they represent. They're often used to compare groups over time or rank discrete things by some numeric measure (country on the x axis and population on the y axis, for example). For time series, a line chart can be a better choice.

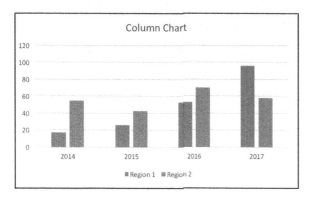

Stacked column charts display the results of multiple data series, combined and stacked atop one another like towers of blocks. These charts use the same data as regular column charts but emphasize overall effects rather than individual values. It's usually a bad idea to try to estimate or compare the individual values (different colors) within the columns of this type of chart.

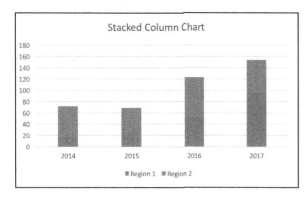

A **100% stacked column chart** compares the percentage that each value contributes to a total across categories. Use this chart when you have two or more data series and you want to emphasize the contributions to the whole, especially if the total is the same for each category.

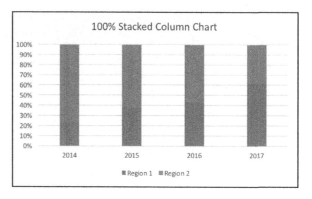

Line charts

Line charts display data series as points connected by straight line segments. They're often used to show trends over time. If you've got a lot of points to plot, line charts are a cleaner and more compact alternative to column charts. A line chart overloaded with five or more lines (data series) is a "spaghetti" chart.

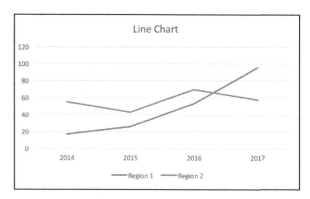

Stacked line and **100% stacked line** charts are also available, and are similar to their counterpart column charts.

Pie charts

A **pie chart** is a circle divided into slices, with each slice showing a percentage of the whole. (Technically, the arc length of each sector of the circle—and consequently its area—is proportional to the value it represents.) Pies show proportions, not specific data values, so they work best for graphing a single row or column with few cells. Despite their popularity, pie charts are usually a bad choice. It's hard to compare different slices of a pie, particularly those with similar values (and forget about comparing data across different pies). They're not bad if you want to compare the size of a single slice to the whole pie, but you're almost always better off with a single-series column chart, or even a non-graphical table of values.

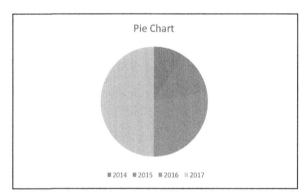

Pie of pie and **bar of pie** charts show pie charts with smaller values pulled out into a secondary pie or stacked bar chart. Use these chart types when you want to make small slices in the main pie chart easier to distinguish.

Bar charts

Bar charts, also called clustered bar charts, are column charts turned sideways (that is, with their axes swapped). They're often used to compare the speed or duration of events. Bar charts look best when you hide the x axis and display the values at the end of each bar.

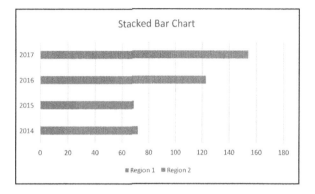

Stacked bar charts are like stacked column charts, only sideways, and with the same caveats.

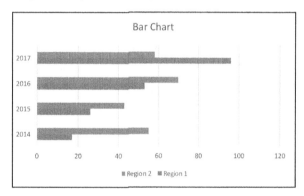

A **100% stacked bar** chart is also available, and is similar to its counterpart 100% stacked column chart.

Area charts

Area charts are like line charts but fill in the space below each line (data series) with a different color. Like line charts, they're often used to show trends over time. The chief danger of area charts is that data series can cross and obscure each other.

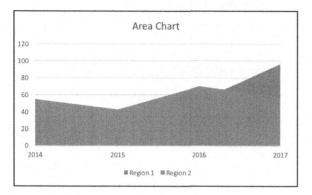

Like stacked column and bar charts, **stacked area charts** emphasize overall effects rather than individual values. The continuous color and joined line segments "flow" rightward across the chart, so they're better than stacked column charts for comparing groups over time. Unlike regular area charts, stacked area charts pose no danger of obscured data points.

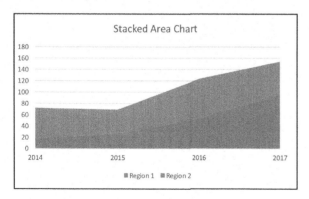

A **100% stacked area** chart is also available, and is similar to its counterpart 100% stacked column chart.

XY (scatter) charts

A **scatter chart** (also called a scatterplot) displays data differently from the other types of charts: it plots every data point on its own x and y coordinates. A scatter chart has two value axes and needs at least two columns or rows of continuous numeric data to plot values for a single data series. To show multiple data series, add columns or rows of y values. Different series of y values are all plotted against the same series of x values; the x data series must be in the first row or column of the chart data. Each pair of data values determines the position of one data point: the first value determines the point's position on the x axis, and the second determines its position on the y axis. Because scatter charts have no category axis, don't convert other types of charts (which don't use paired, or bivariate, data) to scatter charts, or vice versa.

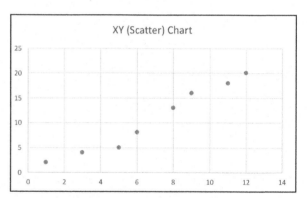

3-D charts

Three-dimensional versions of most of the 2-D chart types are available. 3-D charts obscure and distort data and are generally regarded as useless and amateurish—stick with 2-D charts.

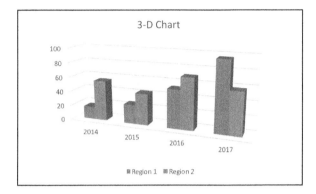

Other types of charts

Stock chart. A stock chart typically is used to show the fluctuation of stock or asset prices over time, but can also be used for scientific data. You can use a stock chart to show the fluctuation of daily rainfall or annual temperatures, for example. You must organize your data in the correct order to create stock charts. To create a simple high-low-close stock chart, for example, arrange your data with High, Low, and Close entered as column headings, in that order. The valid stock charts are high-low-close, open-high-low-close, volume-high-low-close, and volume-open-high-low-close.

Surface chart. A surface chart shows a three-dimensional surface that connects a set of data points, and is useful for finding interesting combinations of two sets of data. As in a topographic map, the colors and patterns in a surface chart indicate areas that contain the same range of values. Unlike other chart types, a surface chart doesn't use colors to distinguish the data series—instead, colors distinguish values that fall in the same band. To enhance a surface chart, you can use transparency to display color bands that are obscured in the back of the chart. Data that's arranged in columns or rows can be plotted in a surface chart. Both categories and data series must be numeric values.

Doughnut chart. Like a pie chart, a doughnut chart shows the relationship of parts to a whole, but it can contain more than one data series. Doughnut charts aren't easy to read. You may want to use a stacked column or stacked bar chart instead. Data that's arranged in columns or rows can be plotted in a doughnut chart.

Bubble chart. A bubble chart resembles a scatter chart, but adds a third column to specify the size of the bubbles it shows to represent the data points in the data series.

Radar chart. A radar chart, also called a spider chart, compares the aggregate values of several data series. Radar charts are often used for quality-control assessments, and for charting sports players' strengths and weaknesses. Data that's arranged in columns or rows can be plotted in a radar chart.

Combo chart. A combo chart uses two chart types (such as line and column) to emphasize that the chart contains different kinds of information. When the range of values for different data series in your chart varies widely, or when you have mixed types of data, you can plot one or more data series from a different chart type on a secondary y axis. You can create combo charts in Excel for Windows or Mac.

Creating a Chart

To create a chart, you start by entering and selecting the numeric data for the chart in a worksheet. Then you can plot that data as a chart by choosing the desired chart type on the Insert tab. You can change, hide, or delete a chart's data series at any time. If the selected chart data has row or column headers, Excel uses the header text as axis and legend labels.

To add a chart to a worksheet:

1. In the worksheet, arrange the data that you want to plot in a chart.

    You can arrange the data in rows or columns—Excel determines the best way to plot the chart data automatically. Some chart types (such as pie and bubble charts) require a specific data arrangement. For details, see "Chart data" on page 116.

2. Select the cells containing the data that you want to use for the chart (Figure 7.1).

    If you select only one cell, Excel expands the selection automatically to chart any data that's in adjacent cells. You can also hide or filter the rows or columns that you don't want to plot in the chart.

3. On the Insert tab, tap Charts to create a specific type of chart (Figure 7.2), or tap Recommended to see a list of charts that Excel recommends for your data (Figure 7.3). For details, see "Picking a Chart Type" on page 119.

4. When you find the chart type that you want, tap it.

    Excel creates the chart on the worksheet (Figure 7.4), and the Chart contextual tab appears in the ribbon.

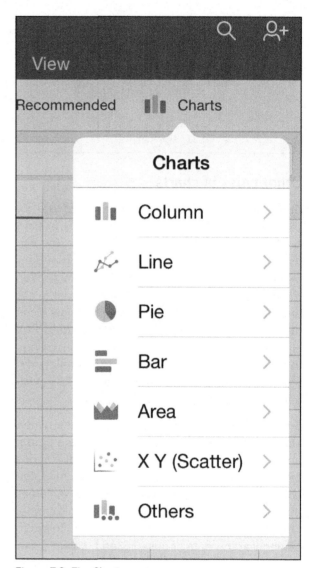

Figure 7.1 Selected cells to use for a chart.

Figure 7.2 The Charts menu.

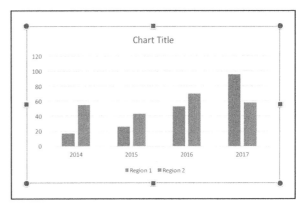

Figure 7.4 A newly created chart.

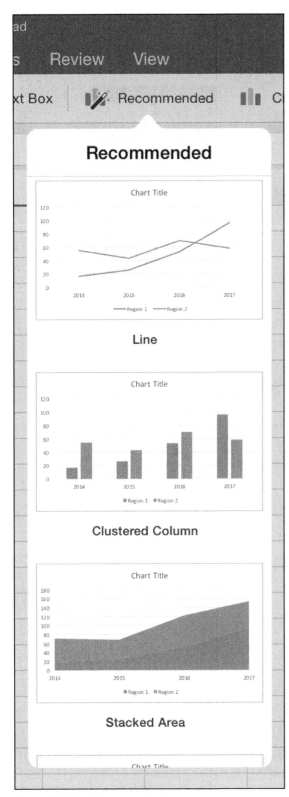

Figure 7.3 The Recommended menu.

Formatting a Chart

You can change a chart's location, size, type, style, color scheme, layout, title, and more. Experiment to learn the effects of the options: change them and watch how the chart updates.

To format a chart:

1 Tap the chart to select it (Figure 7.5).

   When a chart is selected, selection handles ■ and ● appear on the chart's border, the Chart contextual tab appears in the ribbon, the chart's pop-up menu opens, and the chart data is highlighted in the worksheet.

2 Do any of the following:

   ▸ To move the chart, drag it.

   ▸ To resize the chart, drag a selection handle on the chart's border.

   ▸ To change which data is plotted in the chart, find the chart data on a worksheet and then drag the selection handles to encompass the desired range (Figure 7.6). (Selection handles appear on the chart data only when the linked chart is selected.) You can also hide or filter the rows or columns that you don't want to plot in the chart.

   ▸ To change the chart's type, tap Recommended or Types on the Chart tab (Figure 7.7).

   ▸ To format the chart, tap Layouts, Elements, Colors, or Styles on the Chart tab.

   ▸ To swap (transpose) rows and columns as data series, tap Switch on the Chart tab.

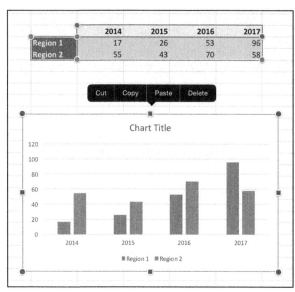

Figure 7.5 A selected chart, with highlighted chart data.

Figure 7.6 Drag the selection handles to change which data is plotted in the chart.

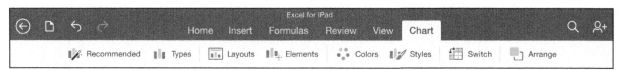

Figure 7.7 The Chart tab.

126   Excel for iPad & iPad Pro

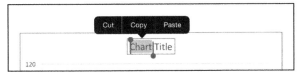

Figure 7.8 Editing a chart title.

- To layer the chart above or below other objects in the stacking order, tap Arrange on the Chart tab.

- To edit a chart title or axis title (Figure 7.8), double-tap the title and then enter a new title by using the standard text selection and editing commands (see "Editing Cells" on page 52).

To cut, copy, or delete a chart:

1. Tap the chart to select it, and then tap Cut, Copy, or Delete on the pop-up menu.

   Cut removes the chart so that it can be moved (pasted) elsewhere. Copy copies a chart so that it can be duplicated (pasted) elsewhere, leaving the original chart intact. Delete removes the chart (without placing a copy on the clipboard).

2. To paste a cut or copied chart, go to the destination (which can be on the same worksheet, on a different worksheet, or on a worksheet in a different workbook), tap an empty area on the worksheet, and then tap Paste on the pop-up menu.

   Pasted charts within the same workbook still reference their original chart data. If you paste a chart in a different workbook file or a different app (such as PowerPoint and Word), Excel severs the chart's links to the original chart data.

Tip: Deleting chart data from a worksheet severs any links that it has to charts, which then revert to placeholder charts.

Chart Layouts and Elements

You can apply a predefined layout to a chart or fine-tune chart elements individually. Select a chart and then tap Layouts or Elements on the Charts tab. You can show, hide, reposition, or reformat chart elements, including:

- Axes
- Axis titles
- Chart title
- Data labels
- Data table
- Error bars
- Gridlines
- Legend
- Lines
- Trendline
- Up/down bars
- Data points and connecting lines
- Bar width and overlap

CHAPTER 8

Pictures, Shapes, Text Boxes, and Add-Ins

You can embellish your worksheets with:

- Photos
- Illustrations
- Geometric Shapes
- Lines
- Arrows
- Symbols
- Callouts
- Text boxes
- Add-ins

Creating Objects

An **object** is any item that you add to a worksheet and can manipulate. Pictures, shapes, text boxes, and add-ins are objects, as are charts.

All objects other than pictures (photos, illustrations, and other static images) are built in to Excel. You can use photos taken with iPad 2 or later, or import photos directly from a digital camera, iPhone, iPod touch, or SD memory card by using the Lightning to SD Card Camera Reader, Lightning to USB Camera Adapter, or (for the iPad 3 or earlier) Apple iPad Camera Connection Kit. To sync photos with your computer, use iTunes. The iPad and Excel support standard image formats: JPEG, TIFF, GIF, and PNG. Synchronizing with iTunes is covered in the *iPad User Guide* at *help.apple.com/ipad*.

To add a picture to a worksheet:

1 Tap Pictures on the Insert tab (Figure 8.1).

   The Photos menu opens. Tap an album or flick up or down to see all the pictures.

2 When you find the picture that you want, tap it.

   Excel adds the picture to the worksheet, and the Picture contextual tab appears in the ribbon.

3 To move the picture, drag it.

Tip: To snap a photo with your iPad's camera and add it to the worksheet, tap Insert tab > Camera.

To add a shape to a worksheet:

1 Tap Shapes on the Insert tab (Figure 8.2).

   The Shapes menu opens. Flick up or down to see all the options. Shapes include geometric shapes, lines, arrows, symbols, and callouts (you can use callouts to point to and explain important results).

2 When you find the shape that you want, tap it.

   Excel adds the shape to the worksheet, and the Shape contextual tab appears in the ribbon.

3 To move the shape, drag it.

To add a text box to a worksheet:

1 Tap Text Box on the Insert tab.

   Excel adds the text box to the worksheet, and the Shape contextual tab appears in the ribbon.

2 To move the text box, drag it.

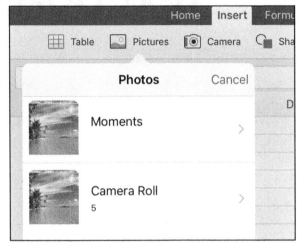

Figure 8.1 The Photos menu.

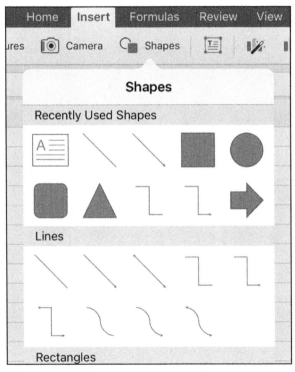

Figure 8.2 The Shapes menu.

Working with Pictures

After adding a picture to a worksheet, you can move it, resize it, format it, and more.

To work with a picture:

1. Tap the picture to select it (Figure 8.3).

   When a picture is selected, selection handles ■ and ● and a rotation handle ↻ appear on the picture's border, the Picture contextual tab appears in the ribbon, and the picture's pop-up menu opens.

2. Do any of the following:

   ▸ To move the picture, drag it.

   ▸ To resize the picture, drag a selection handle on the picture's border. Drag a corner handle ● to resize proportionally or an edge handle ■ to resize freely (which distorts the picture).

   ▸ To format the picture, tap Styles, Shadow, or Reflection on the Picture tab.

   ▸ To layer the picture above or below other objects in the stacking order, tap Arrange on the Picture tab.

   ▸ To crop the picture, tap Crop on the Picture tab.

   ▸ To remove applied formatting and revert to the original picture, tap Reset on the Picture tab.

   ▸ To rotate the picture, drag its rotation handle ↻ clockwise or counter-clockwise. You can rotate to any angle. During rotation, the picture will snap into position at 90-degree increments.

   ▸ To cut, copy, or delete a picture, tap Cut, Copy, or Delete on the pop-up menu. Cut or copied pictures can be pasted elsewhere on the same worksheet, on a different worksheet, on a worksheet in a different workbook, or in a different app (such as Word or PowerPoint).

   ▸ To copy a picture's format to another picture, tap the picture whose format you want to copy, tap Copy on the pop-up menu, tap another picture, and then tap Paste Format on the pop-up menu. Pasting formats is faster than repeatedly slogging through formatting commands on the Picture tab.

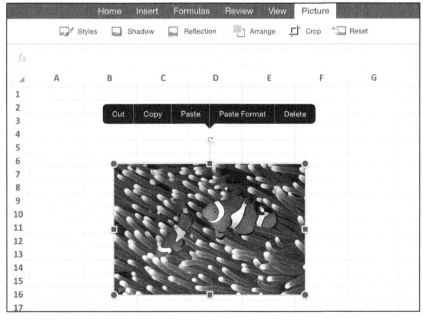

Figure 8.3 A selected picture.

Working with Shapes and Text Boxes

After adding a shape or text box to a worksheet, you can add text to it, move it, resize it, format it, and more.

To work with a shape or text box:

1. Tap the shape or text box to select it (Figure 8.4).

   When a shape or text box is selected, selection handles ■ and ● and a rotation handle ⟳ appear on the object's border, the Shape contextual tab appears in the ribbon, and the object's pop-up menu opens.

2. Do any of the following:

   ▸ To move the object, drag it.

   ▸ To resize the object, drag a selection handle on the object's border. Drag a corner handle ● to resize proportionally or an edge handle ■ to resize freely.

▸ To format the object, tap Shape Styles, Fill, or Outline on the Shape tab.

▸ To insert and edit WordArt, tap WordArt Styles on the Shape tab.

▸ To layer the object above or below other objects in the stacking order, tap Arrange on the Shape tab.

▸ To rotate the object, drag its rotation handle ⟳ clockwise or counter-clockwise. You can rotate to any angle. During rotation, the object will snap into position at 90-degree increments.

▸ To cut, copy, or delete an object, tap Cut, Copy, or Delete on the pop-up menu. Cut or copied objects can be pasted elsewhere on the same worksheet, on a different worksheet, on a worksheet in a different workbook, or in a different app (such as Word or PowerPoint).

Figure 8.4 A selected shape.

Figure 8.5 Select specific text in an object to format it.

- To copy an object's format to another object, tap the object whose format you want to copy, tap Copy on the pop-up menu, tap another object, and then tap Paste Format on the pop-up menu. Pasting formats is faster than repeatedly slogging through formatting commands on the Shape tab.

- To edit text in the object, double-tap the object or tap Edit Text on the pop-up menu, and then enter text by using the standard text selection and editing commands (see "Editing Cells" on page 52).

- To format all the text in the object, tap the object and then use the formatting commands on the Home tab (see "Formatting and Styling Cells" on page 59). To format specific text in the object, double-tap the object or tap Edit Text on the pop-up menu, select the text that you want to format, and then apply formatting (Figure 8.5).

- To reshape the object, drag its yellow selection handles ●, if present (Figure 8.6).

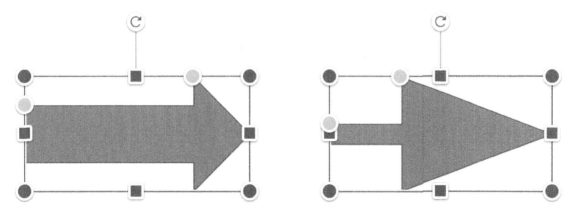

Figure 8.6 Objects that have yellow selection handles can be reshaped.

Chapter 8   Pictures, Shapes, Text Boxes, and Add-Ins   133

Working with Add-Ins

Add-ins are optional components that extend Excel by providing new features. By default, add-ins aren't available in Excel until you download and install them. Add-ins created by Microsoft and third-party developers are available. Microsoft's Bing Maps add-in, for example, lets you plot location data from a given column on a Bing Map, and provides basic data visualization using your location data.

To install an add-in:

1. Tap Add-ins the Insert tab (Figure 8.7).

2. Tap a recommended add-in.

   or

   Tap See All to list all available add-ins, and then tap an add-in (Figure 8.8).

3. Read about how the add-in works with your data. If its actions are acceptable to you, tap the Trust button.

4. Use the add-in in your workbook (Figure 8.9).

   Controls and features vary by add-in.

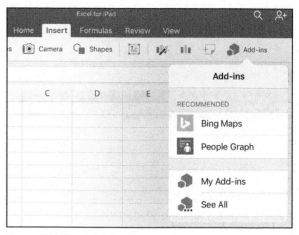

Figure 8.7 The Add-ins menu.

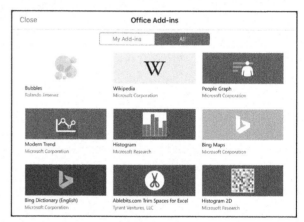

Figure 8.8 The Office Add-ins gallery.

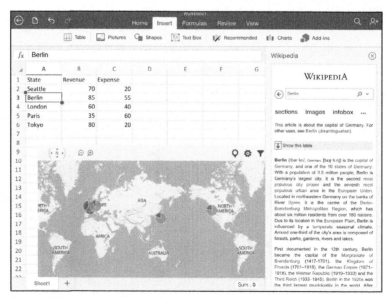

Figure 8.9 You can install multiple add-ins at the same time.

Index

Symbols
& (concatenation operator) 87
# (error values) 99
' (force text) 62
(in narrow columns) 98
: (range operator) 80
<space> (intersection operator) 80
, (union operator) 80

A
absolute cell references 96
add-ins 134
Apple ID 7
App Store 7
arguments, function 89, 91
arithmetic operators
   about 74
   associativity 78
   evaluation order 78
   precedence 78
AutoFit rows and columns 47
AutoSum 92

B
Back button 12
backstage view 11
bezel 6
boolean values 86

C
cached workbooks 22
Calculate Now (F9) 72
cell references
   about 79
   absolute 96
   circular references 98
   formats 81
   inserting 82
   named ranges 84
   relative 96
cells
   about 41
   cell references 79
   clearing 52
   copying 64
   cutting 64
   deleting 44
   editing 52
   filling with data series 68
   finding and replacing content 57
   formatting 59
   formula cells 71
   inserting 44
   merging 66
   moving from cell to cell 52
   named ranges 84
   pasting 64
   selecting 42
   styling 59
   wrapping text in 63
charts 115–128
   about 116
   category axis 118
   chart area 116
   copying 127
   creating 124
   cutting 127
   data points 118
   data series 118
   deleting 127
   elements 127
   formatting 126
   gridlines 118
   layouts 127
   legend 118
   moving 126
   resizing 126
   source data 116, 126
   titles 127
   transposing 118, 126
   types of 119, 126
   value axis 118
   x axis 118
   y axis 118
circular references 98
clipboard 54
cloud storage 19. *See also* **OneDrive**
columns. *See also* **rows**
   about 41
   AutoFit 47
   copying 46
   deleting 44
   freezing 48
   gridlines 41
   headings 79
   hiding 49
   inserting 44
   moving 46
   resizing 47
   selecting 43
   unhiding 49
comments 58
comparison operators 85
computer storage 16
concatenation operator (&) 87
contextual tabs 14

D
data series 68
Dropbox 19

E

errors in formulas 98
error values 98
evaluation order 78
Excel
   add-ins 134
   App Store 7
   Back button 12
   backstage view 11
   basics 8
   clipboard 54
   deleting sign-in credentials 10
   Excel Online 20
   features overview 3
   File menu 12
   file storage
      computer 16
      Dropbox 19
      iCloud Drive 19
      local 16
      OneDrive 19
   installing 7
   Microsoft account 8
   Office 365 account 8
   Office 365 subscriptions 2
   opening 9
   premium features 2
   printing 26
   ribbon 12
   sharing files 24
   signing in 8
   signing out 10
   supported file types 30
   undo/redo 12
   using without signing in 10
   vs. Excel for Windows 8
   workbooks 31
   working offline 21
   workspace 28
Excel Online 20

F

File menu 12
files, supported types 30
folders 34
formula bar 73
formula cells 71
formulas
   about 71, 72
   arithmetic operators 74
   AutoSum 92
   cell references 79
   circular references 98
   comparison operators 85
   constants 74
   copying 94
   entering 76
   equal sign 74
   errors 98
   error values 98
   evaluation order 78
   formula bar 73
   functions 88
   moving 94
   parts of 74
   recalculating 72
   reference operators 80
   saving 77
   using in tables 113
   viewing 73
functions
   about 71, 88
   arguments 89, 91
   commonly used 88
   error values 98
   inserting 90
   optional arguments 91
   syntax 89

G

gridlines, worksheet 41

H

Home screen 4

I

iCloud Drive 19
images. *See* pictures
installing Excel 7
intersection operator (space) 80
iPad
   bezel 6
   Home screen 4
   local storage 16
   multitasking 5
   multitouch gestures 6
   status bar 29

K

keyboards
   configuring 53
   external 56
   onscreen 52
   typing on 53

L

local storage 16
logical operators 85
logical values 86

M

Microsoft account 8
Microsoft Excel. *See* Excel
multitasking 5
multitouch gestures 6

N

named ranges (cells) 84

O

objects, worksheet 129–134
Office 365 account 8
Office 365 subscriptions
   about 2
   deleting sign-in credentials 10
   Microsoft account 8
   Office 365 account 8
   premium features 2
   types of 2
OneDrive
   about 19
   connecting to 20
   OneDrive app 19
   OneDrive.com 19
   OneDrive for Business 20
   recycle bin 37
   resolving editing conflicts 23
   working offline 21
OS X 7

P

photos. *See* pictures
pictures 130, 131
pinning workbooks 22, 32
PowerPoint app 1, 54, 127, 132
precedence, operator 78
premium features 2
printing workbooks 26
properties, workbook 36

R

range operator (:) 80
recycle bin 37
reference operators 80
relational operators 85
relative cell references 96
ribbon 12

rows. *See also* columns
    about 41
    AutoFit 47
    copying 46
    deleting 44
    freezing 48
    gridlines 41
    headings 79
    hiding 49
    inserting 44
    moving 46
    resizing 47
    selecting 43
    sorting 70
    unhiding 49

S
saving workbooks 33
shapes 130, 132
sharing files 24
sign-in credentials, deleting 10
signing in to Excel 8
signing out of Excel 10
SkyDrive. *See* OneDrive
sorting
    rows 70
storage, file
    computer 16
    Dropbox 19
    iCloud Drive 19
    local 16
    OneDrive 19

T
tables 101–114
    about 102
    creating 104
    editing 108
    filtering 112
    formatting 106
    navigating 108
    sorting 111
    Total row 110
    using formulas in 113
    vs. databases 101
tabs, ribbon
    about 13
    collapsing 14
    contextual 14
templates, workbook 31
text
    clipboard 54
    editing 54

finding 57
keyboards
    external 56
    onscreen 52
numbers formatted as 62
placeholders 54
replacing 57
selecting 54
typing 53
wrapping in a cell 63
text boxes 130, 132

U
undo/redo 12
union operator (,) 80

V
version history, workbook 36

W
Windows 7
Word app 1, 54, 127, 132
workbooks
    about 31
    add-ins 134
    cached 22
    copying 35
    creating 32
    deleting 35
    emailing 24
    file storage
        computer 16
        Dropbox 19
        iCloud Drive 19
        local 16
        OneDrive 19
    folders 34
    moving 35
    naming 33
    opening 32
    pinning 22, 32
    printing 26
    properties 36
    recalculating 72
    recycle bin 37
    resolving editing conflicts 23
    saving 33
    sharing 24
    templates 31
    version history 36
worksheets
    about 38
    active 38

    adding 38
    add-ins 134
    comments 58
    copying 39
    deleting 39
    gridlines 41
    hiding 40
    moving (reordering) 39
    objects 129–134
    pictures 130, 131
    recalculating 72
    renaming 38
    shapes 130, 132
    switching 38
    tabs 29, 38
    text boxes 130, 132
    unhiding 40
    zooming 40

Z
zooming 40

Made in the USA
Middletown, DE
24 June 2021